T0301035

# SHAKESPEARE'S "THE TEMPEST"

# SHAKESPEARE'S "THE TEMPEST"

A Modern English Translation

WILLIAM SHAKESPEARE

TRANSLATED BY MORGAN D. ROSENBERG

Algora Publishing
New York

Library of Congress Cataloging-in-Publication Data —

Shakespeare, William, 1564-1616.
    Shakespeare's The Tempest : a modern English translation / William
Shakespeare ; translated by Morgan D. Rosenberg.
        pages cm
    ISBN 978-1-62894-024-4 (soft cover : alk. paper) — ISBN 978-1-62894-025-
1 (hard cover : alk. paper) — ISBN 978-1-62894-026-8 (ebook) 1. Fathers and
daughters—Drama. 2. Political refugees—Drama. 3. Shipwreck victims—Drama.
4. Magicians—Drama. 5. Islands—Drama. 6. Spirits—Drama. 7. Shakespeare,
William, 1564-1616. Tempest. I. Rosenberg, Morgan D., 1973- translator. II. Title.
    PR2833.A2R64 2013
    822.3'3—dc23

                        2013027402

Printed in the United States

# TABLE OF CONTENTS

# INTRODUCTION

Shakespeare's *The Tempest* often serves as an introduction to Shakespeare for modern students, although it is typically not given the same weight as, for example, *Hamlet* or *Macbeth*. The reason for choosing *The Tempest* is that the play is both entertaining and includes timeless themes such as redemption, the nature of the soul, magic and the supernatural, and art's imitation of life (and vice versa).

The story itself is clearly drawn from the traditional Italian *commedia dell'arte*. Although the basic plot is not unique, Shakespeare adds a depth to the story that elevates the play to classic status. The traditional *commedia dell'arte* often included a sorcerer and his daughter as primary characters, along with their supernatural attendants and a number of rustic locals who supplied much of the humor. In *The Tempest*, these roles are taken by Prospero, the sorcerer, his daughter Miranda, the spirit Ariel (and fellow, lower-level spirits), and Stephano and Trinculo who drunkenly wander on the island.

The traditional *commedia dell'arte* generally followed certain themes, with prototypical characters. Pantalone, for example, is the wealthy and manipulative father of Isabella, and their relationship is largely based on Pantalone's quest to find an appropriate suitor for Isabella. Shakespeare builds on this basic structure and weaves a complex backstory for Prospero, based on his fall from power, and how, as you will soon read, he and Miranda ended up stranded on a magical island. More than simply securing a good marriage for Miranda, Prospero's path throughout the play is about his redemption, both in terms of his former position and power, and also his redemption as a father.

Stephano and Trinculo's precursors, known as Arlecchino and Brighella, were merely clowns (in the literal sense), provided for simple physical humor. Although Stephano and Trinculo do provide much of the humor in *The Tempest*, getting drunker and drunker as they wander around the island, they are written as real people, each with pasts and definite opinions and character traits.

Prospero's personal story further builds on the relatively simple character of Pantalone by exploring the Renaissance concept of the tripartite soul, which was seen as being divided into the vegetative, sensitive and rational spheres. The primordial monster, Caliban (based on the *commedia*'s Pulcinella, a lecherous Neapolitan hunchback), represents Prospero being forced to interact with, and get in touch with, the base and primitive "vegetative" part of his soul. In more modern psychological terms, Caliban represents the id of his consciousness. Ariel, his magical spirit, capable of seemingly any task and written with a sense of morality, is the higher, "sensitive" part of his soul—his superego. Miranda, who is both Prospero's anchor and clearly the most pragmatic of all of the characters, is his rational soul, his consciousness and his conscience.

Although *The Tempest* is far from being Shakespeare's only play to feature magic, it was certainly somewhat controversial in Shakespeare's England to go one step farther and make Prospero an actual practitioner of magic. It is believed that *The Tempest* was written in 1610–1611, a time when accused occultists were still being burned at the stake. Perhaps it is out of sheer necessity that Shakespeare further develops the character of Prospero (beyond the simple mage Pantalone) by making the distinction that Prospero was a rational—or, at least, abstract—magician, not an occultist. He does this by clearly contrasting Prospero with Caliban's witch mother, Sycorax, who is described as a devil worshipper. Similarly, Ariel's supernatural nature and powers are contrasted to the evil Sycorax, with Ariel being described as being "too delicate" to carry out Sycorax's evil commands; i.e., although a supernatural creature, Ariel has a basic morality that a demon or other occult creature would lack.

With regard to the theater itself, *The Tempest* is a play full of grand illusion, direct references to the theater and art, and it uses Ariel to summon numerous characters from Greek mythology and theater, including nymphs, harpies and the goddess Ceres. It is interesting to note that numerous later critics, such as Thomas Campbell in 1838, viewed the allusions to the theater as an indication that Prospero was meant to represent Shakespeare himself. When Prospero renounces his magic at the end of the play, this may have represented Shakespeare's farewell to the stage.[1]

---

1 It is widely believed that *The Tempest* is the last play that Shakespeare wrote alone.

One prominent example of Prospero's meta-reference to actors and the theater itself (and, in fact, to Shakespeare's own Globe Theater), is in Act IV, Scene 1 of the play. Here, Prospero is explaining the revels the characters have witnessed, and the associated spirit actors who melt into thin air. Note that this speech ends with one of Shakespeare's most famous quotes:

> "Our revels now are ended. These our actors,
> As I foretold you, were all spirits and
> Are melted into air, into thin air:
> And, like the baseless fabric of this vision,
> The cloud-capp'd towers, the gorgeous palaces,
> The solemn temples, the great globe itself,
> Ye all which it inherit, shall dissolve
> And, like this insubstantial pageant faded,
> Leave not a rack behind. We are such stuff
> As dreams are made on, and our little life
> Is rounded with a sleep."

"We are such stuff as dreams are made on" is just one of the famous quotes in *The Tempest*. As with many of Shakespeare's works, certain lines have become part of our language, remaining in use continuously from the 17th century onward. For example, in Act V, Scene 1, Miranda famously declares,

> "How beauteous mankind is! O brave new world,
> That has such people in't!"

Aldous Huxley named his novel *Brave New World* after this line.

In Act II, Scene 1, Shakespeare writes, "What's past is prologue," a line which is often repeated in modern literature and is even engraved on the National Archives Building in Washington, DC. And, of course, speaking of politics, we are all familiar with the quote, "Politics makes for strange bed-fellows." This saying evolved from a line in Act II, Scene 2, in which Trinculo states (in reference to Caliban), "Misery acquaints a man with strange bedfellows."

The Tempest did not attract much attention before the closing of English theaters in 1642[1]; it only gained popularity after the Restoration, and then only in adapted versions. In the mid-19th century, theater productions began to reinstate the original Shakespearean text, and in the 20th century, critics and scholars undertook a significant re-appraisal of the play's value, leading to the current view that it is one of Shakespeare's greatest works. As a result, The Tempest has inspired at least 46 operas, countless songs, poetry such as Percy Bysshe Shelley's "With a Guitar, To Jane" and W. H. Auden's "The Sea and the Mirror," numerous novels and paintings, and even the classic 1956 science fiction movie Forbidden Planet.

The present work is a modern interpretation of The Tempest based on the 1993 edition of The Tempest from the World Library's Complete Works of William Shakespeare (http://www.gutenberg.org/cache/epub/1135/pg1135.html). This version was selected due to its wide availability, particularly in education. Unlike many of Shakespeare's other plays, The Tempest has changed very little since its first printing. The text, in its current form, was first published in Shakespeare's First Folio in December of 1623. This printing includes more stage directions than any of Shakespeare's other plays, leading scholars over the years to suggest that, as editors of the First Folio, John Heminges and Henry Condell added the directions to the folio to aid the reader and that they were not necessarily

---

1 The Puritans gained control of London early in the English Civil War and ordered the closure of the London theaters on September 2, 1642, on moral grounds.

what Shakespeare originally intended for a stage play. Scholars have also wondered about the masque in Act 4, which seems to have been added as an afterthought, possibly in honor of the wedding of Princess Elizabeth and Frederick V in 1613. However, other scholars see this as unlikely, arguing that to take the masque out of the play creates more problems than it solves. Other than this particular issue, *The Tempest*, in most modern editions and printings, differs very little from the original 1610–1611 version penned by Shakespeare himself.

It is hoped that this modern translation will bring a new audience to *The Tempest* and will inspire continued interest in and future study of this masterpiece.

# CHARACTERS

ALONSO: The King of Naples

SEBASTIAN: Alonso's brother

PROSPERO: The rightful Duke of Milan who was usurped
and exiled by his brother, Antonio. He is also a powerful
magician, controlling nature and having powerful spirits
under his control.

ANTONIO: Prospero's brother, who betrayed Prospero to become the Duke of Milan himself

FERDINAND: Son of Alonso and heir to the throne of Naples

GONZALO: An elderly, noble and honest royal counselor

ADRIAN: A young lord

FRANCISCO: A lord

CALIBAN: Prospero's slave on the island. He is half-monster
and half-human, described as looking something like a
fish.

TRINCULO: A court jester

STEPHANO: A drunken royal butler

SHIPMASTER: Ship's captain

BOATSWAIN: A boatswain on the ship

SAILORS: Assorted sailors

MIRANDA: Prospero's beautiful and innocent daughter

ARIEL: A fairy or spirit in the service of Prospero. The character's gender is not necessarily clear, but Ariel is referred to as "him" in the original play.

IRIS: A Greek goddess, the messenger of the gods. She is impersonated here by one of Prospero's spirits.

CERES: The Roman goddess of agriculture. She is impersonated here by one of Prospero's spirits.

JUNO: The Roman goddess of marriage and queen of the gods. She is impersonated here by one of Prospero's spirits.

NYMPHS: Assorted female nature deities, impersonated here by Prospero's spirits.

REAPERS: Assorted field workers, impersonated here by Prospero's spirits.

OTHER SPIRITS: Various supernatural attendants of Prospero

OTHERS: Various other members of the royal court

# ACT I

SCENE 1: A ship at sea. A raging storm, including
thunder and lightning. The conditions are the
eponymous tempest.)

(A SHIPMASTER and a BOATSWAIN enter.)

SHIPMASTER
Boatswain!

BOATSWAIN
I'm here, sir. What do you need?

SHIPMASTER
Boatswain, go and bolster the sailors. Do it quickly or we
will run aground. Get to it, get to it.

(The SHIPMASTER exits. Enter SAILORS)

BOATSWAIN
Come on, men! That's it, guys! Quickly, quickly! Take in

the topsail. Follow the captain's orders. Blow until you burst, storm, as long as there's enough sea between us and the shore.

(Enter ALONSO, SEBASTIAN, ANTONIO, FERDINAND, GONZALO and OTHERS)

ALONSO
Be careful, boatswain. Where's the captain? Get these men working.

BOATSWAIN
Please stay below, I beg you.

ANTONIO
Where is the captain, boatswain?

BOATSWAIN
Can't you hear him giving orders? You're getting in our way and helping the storm in its battle against us. Please return to your cabins.

GONZALO
Calm down and have some patience.

BOATSWAIN
I will calm down when the sea calms down. Now go! Do you think these waves care about royalty? To your cabins! Shut up and leave us alone.

GONZALO
Listen, my good man, remember who you have aboard.

BOATSWAIN
Nobody I love more than myself. You're the king's advisor, if you have the power to command this storm to cease and return the calm seas, then we will gladly lay down our ropes. Go ahead, use your authority. If that doesn't work, then give thanks that you've lived this long, and go to your cabin to make your peace, if it comes to that. (To SAILORS) Harder, men! (To GONZALO) Now, I'm telling you, get out of our way.

(The BOATSWAIN exits.)

GONZALO
Having spoken to the boatswain, I feel much better. I don't think he will ever drown. Rather, he looks like he's destined to be hanged. Please, Fate, let him make it to his own hanging. Let his hanging rope save us, since our own ropes seem to be doing very little good right now. If I'm wrong and he wasn't born to be hanged, our fate is surely terrible.

(GONZALO exits, along with ALONSO, SEBAS-TIAN, ANTONIO, FERDINAND and OTHERS. Re-enter BOATSWAIN)

BOATSWAIN
Bring down the topmast! Quickly, lower, lower! Bring the main sail in line with the wind! (A shout is heard offstage) Curse those men down there! They are louder than either the storm or us up here. (SEBASTIAN, ANTONIO and GONZA-LO re-enter) Again? What do want? Do you want us to give in to the storm and drown?

SEBASTIAN
I hope you die of throat cancer, you loud, blasphemous, un-grateful dog!

BOATSWAIN
If you want to be up here then get to work!

ANTONIO
Hang, you mongrel dog. Hang, you bastard insolent noise-maker. We're less afraid to be drowned than you are.

GONZALO
I'll guarantee he won't drown, even if the ship is no stronger than a peanut shell and leaking like a woman on her period.

BOATSWAIN
Into the wind, into the wind! Steer her out to sea!

(Enter SAILORS, soaking wet from the storm)

SAILORS
It's over! Pray for your lives! It's all over!

(The SAILORS exit.)

BOATSWAIN
Must we die?

GONZALO
The King and Prince are praying! We should join them. Our fates are entwined with theirs.

SEBASTIAN
I am out of patience.

ANTONIO
We've been cheated out of our lives by a bunch of drunk sailors! (Indicating BOATSWAIN) This big-mouthed rascal here – I hope you drown ten times over!

GONZALO
Despite this storm, I guarantee he'll hang!

(Voices and confusion are heard from offstage: "God have mercy on us! The hull has split open! Farewell, my wife and children! Farewell, brother! The hull is wide open!")

ANTONIO
We go down with the King.

SEBASTIAN
We should say goodbye to him.

(ANTONIO and SEBASTIAN exit.)

GONZALO
Right now, I would trade a thousand miles of sea for just one acre of dry ground. Anything, weeds, dry scrub, anything. It's God's will that we die, but I wish it could have at least been a dry death.

(All exit.)

# ACT I

SCENE 2: The Island, in front of PROSPERO'S
chambers.

(Enter PROSPERO and MIRANDA.)

MIRANDA
Father, if this terrible storm is the result of your magic,
please let it calm down now. It's so dark that it looks like hot
tar might be pouring out of the sky, only the water is so high
that the fire for heating the tar would be put out. Watching
those poor men on the ship suffer like that has also made me
suffer. What a ship, and it must have had at least one good
man aboard, and now all are dashed to pieces! Their screams
tore my heart to pieces! Those poor men, all dead. If I had the
power, I would have drained the ocean before it could swal-
low up the ship and its crew.

PROSPERO
Calm down, it's all over. Trust me, there's no harm done.

MIRANDA
Oh, curse this day!

PROSPERO
No harm at all. Everything I did today, I did for you, my dear daughter. I've kept things from you so that you never knew who I really am and, by extension, who you really are. But, today you will learn that I'm not just poor little Prospero, living in a shack on a wretched little island.

MIRANDA
I never knew there was any more to you, or me, than this.

PROSPERO
It's time that I tell you the truth. Help me take off this magic cloak. (MIRANDA helps PROSPERO take off his cloak, which they lay down on the ground.) Lie there, my magic. Now, wipe your eyes and calm down. Despite the shipwreck you just saw, and which caused you to get so upset, I am so skillful in magic that I safely managed the whole thing without harming even a single hair on anyone's head. Now, sit down and I'll tell you my story.

MIRANDA
So many times, you have started to tell me who I really am, but then you just stopped, leaving me puzzling, not saying anything else other than, 'Wait. Not yet.'

PROSPERO
Well, the time has finally come. Listen to me carefully. Do you remember a long time ago, before we ever came here? I doubt if you have any clear memory of that, since you weren't even three years old at the time.

MIRANDA
Yes, father, I remember.

PROSPERO
What do you remember? A house, a person? Tell me anything you can remember from before.

MIRANDA
It's very hazy, like a dream. I seem to remember having four
or five women who took care of me?

PROSPERO
Yes, you had such women, and a lot more, Miranda. I wonder how you remember that. What else do you remember
from before? Do you remember how we came here?

MIRANDA
No, I don't remember that.

PROSPERO
Twelve years ago, Miranda, twelve years ago, your father
was the Duke of Milan and a prince of power.

MIRANDA
Wait, aren't you my father?

PROSPERO
Well, your mother was a virtuous woman and she said that
you were my daughter, so there you have it. Your father was
the Duke of Milan, and you a princess, his only heir.

MIRANDA
Oh my God! What kind of treachery drove us from Milan to

this island? Or was it a blessing, coming here?

PROSPERO
Both horrible and a blessing, my girl. By treachery, as you say, we were driven out, but it was a blessing that we found our way here.

MIRANDA
It breaks my heart to make you tell me this, but I have to hear more.

PROSPERO
My brother, your uncle Antonio – I still can't believe that any brother could be so treacherous – whom I loved more than anyone else, except you of course, I trusted to manage my estate. At the time, my estate was the most powerful in the land, and I was the primary Duke, famous for my dignity and education. However, I was so engrossed in my studies of magic and secret knowledge that I failed to see that my dukedom started to slip. Your double-crossing uncle ... are you paying attention?

MIRANDA
Absolutely.

PROSPERO
Once your uncle learned how to grant favors and requests to some people, how to deny them to others, whom to advance and whom to destroy, he turned my own people against me, changed them. Since I had essentially given him all of my power to run things, he was able to take over all of Milan and

her people – they were soon singing his song. He was like the ivy growing on a tree trunk, sucking the very life out of the tree to become lush and green itself. You're not paying attention!

MIRANDA
Yes I am, father!

PROSPERO
Please listen carefully. I was so dedicated to my solitary studies that I neglected my life and my duties. As an unin-tended consequence of locking myself away, I stirred up the evil, true nature of my brother. Ironically, my deep trust in him is what allowed him to become so untrustworthy. My trust in him, which was boundless, allowed him to be untrustworthy to a similar boundless extent. With my power and wealth now his, plus what he was able to gain on his own, Antonio began to believe he was the real Duke of Milan, rather than simply acting the part. He wore the face of royalty, with all of the power that goes with it. With his ambition growing like this ... are you listening?

MIRANDA
Your story, father, could cure deafness.

PROSPERO
To turn this role he was playing into reality, he simply needed to become the Duke of Milan himself. As for me at this time, my library was dukedom enough for my needs. Thus, Antonio decided I was incapable of carrying out my duties as

Duke. He allied himself with the King of Naples, agreeing to pay him an annual tribute, swear loyalty to him, and put the dukedom of Milan, never before subservient to anyone, under the humiliating control of Naples.

MIRANDA
My God!

PROSPERO
Think about my story and its consequences, and then tell me if this is a man I can call 'brother'.

MIRANDA
It would be wrong of me to think poorly of my grandmoth-er, but sometimes good wombs have borne bad sons.

PROSPERO
Here is the agreement they made: The King of Naples, be-ing an established enemy of mine, listened to my brother's re-quest, which was that he, in exchange for the monetary trib-ute and loyalty given to him – and I don't know how much money it was – would remove both me and those loyal to me from Milan. The title of Duke, and all of its honors and duties, would then go to my brother. In one night, an army of traitors was gathered together, solely for the purpose of removing me and my followers, and Antonio himself opened the gates of Milan. Under the cover of darkness, his officers grabbed me and you, crying in my arms, and took us away.

MIRANDA
How terrible! I don't remember crying that night, so I will cry now. Your story breaks my heart.

PROSPERO

Listen to just a little bit more and we'll be caught up. The present situation is what necessitated this story in the first place.

MIRANDA

Why weren't we killed that night?

PROSPERO

Good question, my daughter! The story begs that question. They didn't kill us that night because I was so beloved by the people of Milan. It was also for this reason that my brother had to hide their treacherous intentions. To make a long story short, they hurried us onto a ship, sailed out a ways, prepared a rotting old boat with no sails, tackle or mast, which even rats wouldn't live on, and set us adrift. We were left with no one but the sea to hear our cries, and the sea roared right back at us. We were left to sigh into the wind, which sighed right back at us out of pity.

MIRANDA

My goodness, what a burden I must have been to you!

PROSPERO

No, you were my angel, constantly saving me! Your smile was infused with precious strength from heaven, given to me whenever I cried my salty tears into the sea and groaned under our burden. Your precious smile raised me up to face any situation.

MIRANDA
How did we come ashore?

PROSPERO
By God's divine will. We had some food and fresh water that a noble Neapolitan, Gonzalo, gave to us out of the goodness of his heart. He had been appointed to carry out the plan against us, but he gave us not only the food and water, but good clothing, linen, supplies and various other necessities, all of which have been such a great help ever since. Knowing how I loved my books, he also provided the most valuable volumes from my library.

MIRANDA
I wish I could meet that man!

PROSPERO
Let me stand up. (PROSPERO stands and puts on his cloak) Sit still, and listen to the end of the story. We arrived here, on this island, where, acting as your teacher, I have given you a finer education than that of any princess. Most princesses don't have such teachers and waste their time on pure vanity.

MIRANDA
And I am thankful for it! Please, father, I'm still wondering, what was your reason for conjuring this great storm?

PROSPERO
You should know this: Simply by accident, by fate, my daughter, were my enemies brought to this shore. I foresee that my own fate hangs on this event, and if I mishandle

things from here on, it will be the cause of my downfall. Now, stop asking questions, you look tired. Give in to it and go to sleep. (MIRANDA falls asleep) Come, servant, come. I am ready for you now. Approach, my Ariel. Come.

(Enter ARIEL.)

ARIEL

All hail, great master! My worthy master, hail! Your wish is my command. For you, I will fly, swim, dive into fire, ride on the clouds themselves. Simply ask and Ariel will obey.

PROSPERO

Spirit, did you raise the tempest just as I asked?

ARIEL

I followed your instructions to the letter. I boarded the King's ship, moving from top to bottom, across the deck, into every cabin. I appeared as fire, amazing all. Sometimes I'd divide myself and burn in many places: I burned distinctly and simultaneously on the topmast, the yards and the bow. I then joined together into a single flame, like Zeus's lightning, a precursor to the lightning of the storm. The fire and thunder claps overcame even mighty Neptune, making his bold waves tremble and his dread trident shake.

PROSPERO

My brave spirit! Who could possibly be so calm and brave that such a storm would not make him crazy?

ARIEL

Not one of them escaped the madness, not one avoided acting out of desperation. All but the sailors dove into the heaving waves, leaving the ship still burning with the fire that was really me. The King's son, Ferdinand, with his hair standing on end – it looked like reeds rather than hair – was the first overboard, crying, 'Hell is empty, and all the devils are here.'

PROSPERO
Now that's my spirit! Was this near the shore?

ARIEL
Close by, my master.

PROSPERO
Ariel, are they all safe?

ARIEL
Not a hair harmed. Not a stain on a single shirt. Better than new, in fact, fresher than before. And, as you commanded me, I divided them into groups and dispersed them about the island. I placed the King's son by himself, off in a far nook of the island. I left him sitting there, sighing, with his arms sadly wrapped around himself.

PROSPERO
What did you do with the King's ship, its sailors and the rest of the fleet?

ARIEL
They are all safely harbored. The King's ship is hidden in that deep nook where you once called me up at midnight to fetch dew from the stormy Bermuda islands. The sailors are

all asleep below deck, tired from their labors and with just a bit of a magic charm. As for the rest of the fleet, I dispersed them in the surrounding area and they have already all met up with one another in the Mediterranean, sadly bound home to Naples, thinking that they witnessed the death of their King in a shipwreck.

PROSPERO
Ariel, you performed exactly as I asked, but there is more work to do. What time is it?

ARIEL
Past noon.

PROSPERO
It's at least two hours past. The time between now and six o'clock will be most important.

ARIEL
Is there more work to do? Since you are giving me a new assignment, let me remind you of your promise to me, your promise which has not yet been granted.

PROSPERO
Why this new tone? Just what is it you want from me?

ARIEL
My freedom.

PROSPERO
Before your sentence is completed? I don't want to hear any more of this!

ARIEL
I beg you, think about how loyal I have been serving you. I
have never lied to you, I've made no mistakes, I have served
you without complaint, without forming a grudge. You promised to take a year off of my sentence.

PROSPERO
Have you forgotten the torment I freed you from?

ARIEL
No.

PROSPERO
You have. You complain. You think it's such a burden to
walk through the ocean, to ride the sharp north winds, to do
my business in the chasms of the earth when it is cold.

ARIEL
I do not, sir.

PROSPERO
You lie, you awful thing. Have you forgotten the foul witch
Sycorax, all stooped over by age and full of envy? Have you
forgotten her?

ARIEL
No, sir.

PROSPERO
You have. Where was she born? Go ahead, speak, tell me.

ARIEL
Sir, in Algiers.

PROSPERO
Oh, was she? I will have to re-tell you the story, once a month, since you seem to have forgotten it. The damned witch Sycorax was banished from Algiers for her wild mischief and magic, which was so terrible it can't even be spoken of. There was only one single reason they didn't execute her. Isn't that true?

ARIEL
Yes, sir.

PROSPERO
The blue-eyed hag was brought to this island, pregnant, and left here by sailors. You, my slave, as even you admit, were her servant. But you were too innocent, too cowardly to carry out her abhorrent commands. Refusing her orders, she was enraged and imprisoned you, with the aid of her powerful spirits, in a hollow pine tree for twelve years. In that span, she died, leaving you stuck there, groaning over and over again, like a mill wheel going around and around, striking, striking, striking the water. You were all alone, this island was uninhabited except for the son that Sycorax gave birth to, a freckled baby, witch-born, inhuman.

ARIEL
Yes, Caliban, her son.

PROSPERO
That's right, you moron. Caliban, whom I also keep in my

service. Remember the torment I found you in. Your groans made wolves howl, penetrated the hearts of angry bears – your torment was that of the damned, with even Sycorax herself being unable to put an end to it. It was only by my command of magic that, when I came here and heard you, I was able to release you from the pine.

ARIEL
I thank you, master.

PROSPERO
If you complain again, I will split an oak tree and lock you up in its knotty interior until you have howled for another twelve winters.

ARIEL
I am sorry, master. I will obey your commands and do my spiriting without complaint.

PROSPERO
Do so and after just two more days, I will free you.

ARIEL
That's my noble master! What shall I do? Tell me. What shall I do?

PROSPERO
Go make yourself look like a sea nymph. Be invisible to all but you and me. Take this cloak, put it on and then come back here. Quickly, go!

(ARIEL exits with the invisibility cloak given by PROSPE-
RO. For the remainder of the play, whenever ARIEL is wearing the cloak, ARIEL is invisible to all but PROSPERO.)

(To MIRANDA) Wake up, darling, wake up. You had a
good sleep, wake up.

MIRANDA

The strangeness of your story overcame me and made me so
woozy and tired.

PROSPERO

Shake it off. Come on, we'll visit Caliban, my horrible slave.

MIRANDA

He is a villainous monster, father, I can't stand the sight of
him.

PROSPERO

But, as it is, we need him. He makes our fire, fetches our
wood, and serves us in many ways that benefit us. Hey! Slave!
Caliban! You piece of filth! Speak.

CALIBAN

(From within PROSPERO's chambers) You already have
plenty of wood in here.

PROSPERO

I command you to come here, I have something else for you
to do. Come out here, slowpoke! Will you ever get out here?
(ARIEL re-enters, disguised as a water nymph) Ah, what a
fine spirit! My dear Ariel, listen carefully.

(PROSPERO whispers to ARIEL.)

ARIEL
My lord, it shall be done.

(ARIEL exits.)

PROSPERO
You wretched slave, child of the devil, come out here!

(Enter CALIBAN.)

CALIBAN
I hope you both get covered with wicked dew, like the dew my mother brushed from the unwholesome marsh with a raven's feather! May a hot, southwest wind blow on you and scald you all over!

PROSPERO
Just for that, I'll give you cramps tonight, pain in your side so severe that you won't be able to breathe. Goblins will torment you all night. You'll be pinched and stung, stung more severely than by any bee.

CALIBAN
I must eat my dinner. This island's mine, inherited from my mother, Sycorax. You stole it from me. When you first came here, you stroked me, flattered me, you gave me water with berries in it and taught me the names for the sun and the moon. I loved you and showed you this island, from the fresh springs to the saltwater pits, from the barren spots to the

most fertile land. I curse myself for doing this! All the curses of Sycorax, toads, beetles and bats on you! I was king of all of this and now you enslave me. I'm your sole subject in this land, on this hard rock, and you keep me here, away from the rest of the island.

PROSPERO

You are a lying slave, and I've learned the hard way that the only way to motivate you is with the whip and not with kindness! I treated you well, filth that you are, even letting you live in my own chambers until you tried to rape my daughter.

CALIBAN

Oh, if only I had succeeded. If you hadn't stopped me, I would have populated this whole island with little Calibans.

MIRANDA

You horrible slave. You're incapable of learning how to be good. You are only capable of being evil. I pitied you, spent my time teaching you how to speak our language, teaching you so many things each and every day. When you knew nothing, jabbering away like some brute, I helped you find the words to make your thoughts known. Though you learned what I taught you, you were still a vile creature, and good people could not stand being near you. You got what you deserved, being locked up in this cave. It's what you deserve, even prison would be too good for you.

CALIBAN

You taught me language, and now all it's good for is cursing. I curse you for teaching me your language!

PROSPERO

Get out of here, you son of a bitch! Go fetch us firewood. And be quick about it, I have more tasks for you. Are you shrugging me off, you evil thing? If you are lazy or disobedient, I'll inflict cramps on you, make your bones ache, make you scream so loudly that all of the animals on this island will tremble at the noise.

CALIBAN

No, I beg of you. (As an aside) I must obey. His magic is so powerful that it could even control and enslave my mother's god, Setebos.

PROSPERO

Go then, slave!

(Exit CALIBAN. Re-enter ARIEL, invisible, playing and singing. FERDINAND is following ARIEL).

ARIEL (sings this part)
    Come unto these yellow sands,
    And we'll join hands;
    Curtsied when we've kissed,
    The wild waves whist,
    Dance lightly here and there,
    And, sweet sprites, the burden bear.
    Listen, hark!
(Offstage SPIRITS, dispersed in various places, give the refrain: Bow-wow.)
    The watch dogs bark.

(Offstage SPIRITS, dispersed in various places, give the refrain: Bow-wow.)
> Listen, listen! I hear
> The strain of strutting chanticleer
> Crying cock-a-doodle-do.[1]

FERDINAND
Where is this music coming from? From the air or the
ground? It's stopped. It must be for some god of the island.
Sitting on the shore, crying for my drowned father, the King,
and I hear this music come from across the water, calming
both the waves and my own grief with its sweet melody. I
have followed it here or, rather, it drew me here. But now it's
gone. No, it's beginning again.

ARIEL (sings this part)
> Five fathoms below your father lies;
> Of his bones are coral made;
> Those are pearls that were his eyes;
> Nothing of him that does fade
> But does suffer a sea change
> Into something rich and strange.
> Sea nymphs hourly ring his death bell:
(Offstage SPIRITS, dispersed in various places, give the refrain: Ding-dong.)
> Listen!
> Now I hear them, Ding-dong bell.[2]

---

1 Note that only minor translational changes have been made in this passage, as this
 song is intended to rhyme; the original rhyme scheme has been retained.
2 Only minor translational changes have been made; the original rhyme scheme has
 been retained.

FERDINAND
The song references my drowned father. This must be supernatural. Now I hear the music above me.

PROSPERO
(Speaking to MIRANDA) Raise the curtains of your eyelids
and tell me what you see over there.

MIRANDA
(MIRANDA sees FERDINAND) What is it? A spirit? Lord,
it's looking all around! Wow, father, it sure is fine looking.
But it is just one of your spirits.

PROSPERO
No, my girl, it eats and sleeps and has identical senses to
ours. This gentleman who you see before you was in the shipwreck. If he wasn't grieving, which tends to detract from
beauty, you might even call him handsome. He has lost his
friends and is now wandering around, trying to find them.

MIRANDA
I might call him divine. I have never seen such a noble man.

PROSPERO
(As an aside) It's all following my plan, just as I intended.
Spirit, fine spirit! I'll free you within two days for this.

FERDINAND
(FERDINAND sees MIRANDA) This must be the goddess
the music is playing for. I beg you, please tell me if you live
on this island and how I should act here. My main question,

though, which I saved for last, is – oh, you wonder! – are you a woman?

MIRANDA
I'm no wonder, sir, but I am definitely a woman.

FERDINAND
You speak my language? Heavens! I'm the highest ranking person that speaks this language, if only I was back in the land where it's spoken.

PROSPERO
What? The highest ranking person? What would the King of Naples do to you if he heard you?

FERDINAND
He would see me for exactly what I am, a person amazed to hear you speak of Naples. The King does hear me, I'm certain, and that makes me cry. I am now the King of Naples, since I saw with my own eyes, which haven't been dry since, my father, the King, drowned in a shipwreck.

MIRANDA
Oh, how terrible!

FERDINAND
Yes, indeed, and all of his lords, the Duke of Milan and his fine son, too.

PROSPERO
(As an aside) The real Duke of Milan and his even finer

daughter could control you, if it was the right time to do it. It's obviously love at first sight. Delicate Ariel, I'll set you free for this. (To FERDINAND) A word, my good fellow. I'm afraid you've made a mistake. Let me have a word with you.

MIRANDA
Why is my father speaking to him like this? This is only the third man I've ever seen and only the first who has ever made me sigh. I hope my father takes pity on me and treats him well for my sake.

FERDINAND
(To MIRANDA) Oh, if you're still a virgin and not in love with another man, I'll make you the Queen of Naples.

PROSPERO
Hold on, sir! Just one word with you. (As an aside) They are both in each other's power, but I need to create a little challenge here so that this isn't just a lighthearted romp for either of them. (To FERDINAND) One word. I order you to listen to me. You're calling yourself by a false title, and I think you have come here as a spy to steal the island from me, its rightful lord.

FERDINAND
No, I swear on my honor.

MIRANDA
A man as fine as this could not possibly be deceitful. If hell was as beautiful as this man, even the holiest of people would fight to live there.

PROSPERO
(To FERDINAND) Follow me. (To MIRANDA) Don't speak to him, he's a traitor. (To FERDINAND) Come here, I'm going to chain your neck and feet together. You will drink seawater. For food, you'll eat mussels, withered roots and acorn shells. Follow me.

FERDINAND
No. I will resist your imprisonment for as long as I can.

(FERDINAND draws his sword and PROSPERO uses his magic to keep FERDINAND frozen in place.)

MIRANDA
Oh, dear father, don't judge him so quickly. He's gentle and brave.

PROSPERO
What's that? My student has now become my teacher? (To FERDINAND) Put away your sword, traitor. You put on quite a show with your sword, but you dare not use it. Your conscience is full of guilt. Change positions or I will knock your sword out of your hand with this stick (showing his magic staff.)

MIRANDA
I beg you, father!

PROSPERO
Let me go! Don't hang on my robes like that.

MIRANDA

Please, father, take pity on him. I guarantee his virtue.

PROSPERO

Silence! One word more and I'll be forced to punish you, maybe even hate you. What's gotten into you? An advocate for an impostor! Hush! You think he's particularly handsome, but you only have Caliban to compare him with. Foolish girl! To most people, this is another Caliban and, compared with him, the world is full of beautiful angels.

MIRANDA

Then my love is humble. I have no ambition to see a more handsome man than this one.

PROSPERO

(To FERDINAND) Come on, obey me. Your nerve is like that of a baby and your muscles are like jelly.

FERDINAND

So they are. My spirit is all bound up, like in a dream. The death of my father, my physical weakness, the death of all of my friends in the shipwreck, even the threats of this man, who now imprisons me, mean nothing to me if I can look out of my prison, just once a day, and see this beautiful girl. If that were true, I would need no more freedom than that. Such a prison would offer me all the space I could ever need.

PROSPERO

(As an aside) It's working. (To FERDINAND) Come on. (As an aside) You have done well, fine Ariel! (To FERDINAND)

Follow me. (To ARIEL) I have your next command, listen.

MIRANDA
Don't worry, my father is a better man than he appears to be. He is not being his usual self.

PROSPERO
(To ARIEL) You shall be as free as the mountain winds, but you must follow my instructions exactly.

ARIEL
To the syllable.

PROSPERO
(To FERDINAND) Come, follow. (To MIRANDA) Don't try to defend him.

(All exit.)

# ACT II

SCENE 1: Another part of the island

(Enter ALONSO, SEBASTIAN, ANTONIO, GONZALO, ADRIAN, FRANCISCO and OTHERS.)

GONZALO
(To ALONSO) Please, sir, cheer up. Just like the rest of us, you have a good reason to be happy. Escaping our fate is far greater than anything we've lost. Sure, feeling despair for a moment makes sense, but every day, some sailor's wife, a ship's crew, and the merchant who hired the crew go through a wreck like this. But, miraculously, *we* were saved. Only a few out of millions can say that. Remember that, my good friend, and weigh your sadness against our good luck.

ALONSO
Please, stop speaking.

SEBASTIAN
(To ANTONIO) He takes to comforting words like he takes to cold porridge.

ANTONIO
Gonzalo will not give up so easily.

SEBASTIAN
Look, you can see him winding up the gears of his wit, like a clock ready to strike the hour.

GONZALO
(To ALONSO) Sir ...

SEBASTIAN
One o'clock.

GONZALO
If we let every little thing get us down ...

SEBASTIAN
What a pain.

GONZALO
Yes, it is pain that we are feeling. Your words are truer than you intended.

SEBASTIAN
You are taking it more seriously than I meant you to.

GONZALO
(To ALONSO) Therefore, my lord ...

ANTONIO
(To SEBASTIAN) Wow, he never shuts up!

ALONSO
(To GONZALO) I beg you, please, no more.

GONZALO
Well, I'm almost done, just one more thing ...

SEBASTIAN
(To ANTONIO) He just keeps on talking.

ANTONIO
Okay, let's wager. Who will babble next, him or Adrian?

SEBASTIAN
The old fart.

ANTONIO
I choose the kid.

SEBASTIAN
Done. The wager?

ANTONIO
A good laugh.

SEBASTIAN
You're on!

ADRIAN
Though this island seems to be deserted ...

ANTONIO
Ha, ha, ha!

SEBASTIAN
You win and you got your laugh.

ADRIAN
... uninhabitable and almost inaccessible ...
SEBASTIAN
'Yet'?

ADRIAN
Yet ...

ANTONIO
He had to say it. He had to.

ADRIAN
It must have a mild and temperate climate.

ANTONIO
Ah, Temperance, she was a fine woman.

SEBASTIAN
Yes, and she was mild, too, just as he wisely said.

ADRIAN
The gentle breeze is so pleasant here, like a breath of fresh
air.

SEBASTIAN
As if the air had lungs, and rotten ones at that.

ANTONIO
Or as if it was perfumed by a stinky swamp.

GONZALO
Here we find everything we need to live.

ANTONIO
True, except for the 'live' part.
SEBASTIAN
Yes, there's no life here or, at least, very little.

GONZALO
How lush and healthy the grass looks! How green!

ANTONIO
The ground, in fact, is brown.

SEBASTIAN
With just a touch of green in it.

ANTONIO
He certainly doesn't miss much.

SEBASTIAN
No, he just gets things totally wrong.

GONZALO
But the really unbelievable thing is, and this is really incredible ...

SEBASTIAN

As many unbelievable things are.


GONZALO

... that our clothes, being, as they were, drenched in the sea, are somehow still fresh, looking brand new rather than soaked in salt water.


ANTONIO

If only one of his pockets could speak, wouldn't it call him a liar?


SEBASTIAN

Yes or, at least, pocket up this speech.


GONZALO

I think our clothes are now as fresh as when we first put them on in Africa, at the marriage of the King's beautiful daughter, Claribel, to the King of Tunis.


SEBASTIAN

It was a beautiful wedding, and we're certainly doing well on our voyage home.


ADRIAN

Tunis has never before had such a beautiful queen.


GONZALO

Not since the time of the widow Dido.

ANTONIO

Widow! To hell with that! Why are you calling her a 'widow'? The widow Dido!

SEBASTIAN

What if he had said 'the widower Aeneas', too? Good Lord, how you overreact!

ADRIAN

'The widow Dido', you said? I'm not sure about that. She was from Carthage, not Tunis.

GONZALO

Tunis, sir, was Carthage.[1]

ADRIAN

Carthage?

GONZALO

I assure you, Carthage.

ANTONIO

He speaks with such certainty that it can make miracles happen.

SEBASTIAN

He can raise walls and build houses with his words alone.

ANTONIO

---

1 Gonzalo says this with certainty and pomp, though he is incorrect.

What miracle will he work next?

SEBASTIAN
I think he will carry this island home in his pocket, and give it to his son like an apple.

ANTONIO
And, planting the seeds in the sea, grow more islands.

GONZALO
Yes.

ANTONIO
Absolutely yes.

GONZALO
Sir, we were talking about how our clothing now seems as fresh as when we were in Tunis at the wedding of your daughter, the new Queen.

ANTONIO
And the most beautiful Queen they have ever had.

SEBASTIAN
I beg your pardon, except for the widow Dido.

ANTONIO
Oh, the widow Dido! Yes, the widow Dido.

GONZALO
Sir, isn't my jacket as fresh as the first day I wore it? I mean, in a way.

ANTONIO
That 'way' was well fished for.

GONZALO
When I wore it at your daughter's wedding?

ALONSO
You keep talking and cramming these words into my ears,
words that make me sick. I wish I had never held my daughter's wedding there. I lost my son because of it and, in a way,
my daughter, too, since she is now so far from Italy that I'll
never see her again. Oh, my son, heir of Naples and Milan,
what strange fish has made a meal out of you?

FRANCISCO
Sir, he may still be alive. I saw him fight the waves, riding
on top of them. He was able to swim strongly, beating back
the waves, keeping his head above water. He used his strong
arms like oars to bring him to the shore, which seemed eager
to receive him. I have no doubt he made it to shore alive.

ALONSO
No, no, he's gone.

SEBASTIAN
Sir, you have yourself to thank for this great loss. Rather
than blessing Europe with your daughter, you let her go off
with an African. At least she won't be around to remind you
of this current tragedy.

ALONSO
Please, be quiet.

SEBASTIAN
All of us begged you not to go through with it. Your daughter herself struggled between her own reluctance and her obedience to you. I fear that we have lost your son forever. Due to this whole business, Milan and Naples have more widows than we bring in men to comfort them, and it's all your fault.

ALONSO
And the greatest share of grief is mine as well.

GONZALO
My lord Sebastian, though what you say may be true, it's tactless and this is hardly the moment to insist on it. You are rubbing salt in fresh wounds when, instead, you should be applying bandages.

SEBASTIAN
Very well.

ANTONIO
And with the care of a doctor.

GONZALO
(To ALONSO) When there is foul weather in you, sir, there is foul weather in us all.

SEBASTIAN
Foul weather?

ANTONIO
Very foul.

GONZALO
If I could settle on this island, my lord ...

ANTONIO
He'd sow it with weeds.

SEBASTIAN
Or thorn bushes.

GONZALO
And if I were King of this island, do you know what I would do?

SEBASTIAN
He would finally escape being an old drunk due to the island's lack of wine.

GONZALO
In this land, I would do everything the opposite of how it is usually done. There would be no commerce, no officials, no education. There would be no wealth, no poverty, no servants. No contracts, no inheritance, no borders or boundaries for land or farms, no use of metal, corn, or wine, or oil. There would be no work at all, all men would be idle. Women, too. Everyone would be innocent and pure. There would be no royalty ...

SEBASTIAN
Yet he is still the King in a place with no royalty or government.

ANTONIO
The end of his fantasy has forgotten the beginning.

GONZALO
Everything would be produced without effort. There would be no treason, felony, swords, pikes, knives, cannons, or need of any weapon. Nature would provide everything, its harvests in abundance, and that is how my innocent people would be fed.

SEBASTIAN
No marriage among his subjects?

ANTONIO
None at all. Everyone is idle. They would all be whores and slackers.

GONZALO
I would govern so perfectly, sir, that my kingdom would exceed that of the golden age.

SEBASTIAN
Long live his Majesty!

ANTONIO
Long live Gonzalo!

GONZALO
(To ALONSO) Are you listening to me, sir?

ALONSO
I beg you, no more. Your words mean nothing to me.

GONZALO
You are absolutely correct, your Highness. I was simply providing these gentlemen with a laugh. They always find humor in meaningless things.

ANTONIO
It was *you* we were laughing at.

GONZALO
But, in this kind of foolishness, I am meaningless to you, like nothing at all. Thus, you are laughing at meaningless things. Go on, continue to laugh at nothing.

ANTONIO
Oh, what a searing comeback, a real blow!

SEBASTIAN
A blow that fell flat.

GONZALO
You are such brave and strong gentlemen. You would push the moon in her orbit if she were to get stuck in place for five weeks.

(Enter ARIEL, invisible, playing solemn music.)

SEBASTIAN
Yes, we would, and then we would go bird hunting.

ANTONIO
(To GONZALO) My lord, don't be angry with us.

GONZALO
I'm not. I know you've got nothing against me. Will you laugh me to sleep? I am quite tired.

ANTONIO
Go to sleep, and hear us laughing.

(All fall asleep under ARIEL's spell except for ALONSO, SEBASTIAN and ANTONIO.)

ALONSO
Whoa, everyone fell asleep so quickly! I wish that I could also sleep, it would stop this horrible stream of thoughts. Hmm, I *am* feeling sleepy.

SEBASTIAN
Well then, please, sir, give into it. It's rare that someone who is grieving gets to sleep, but when they do, it is often a great comfort.

ANTONIO
My lord, the two of us will guard you while you sleep and make sure you are safe.

ALONSO
Thank you, I'm becoming terribly sleepy!

(ALONSO sleeps. Exit ARIEL.)

SEBASTIAN
It's strange how they all just fell asleep like that!

ANTONIO
It must be something in the air.

SEBASTIAN
Then why isn't it making us sleepy, too? I'm not tired at all.

ANTONIO
Neither am I. I'm wide awake. It was like they all just agreed to fall asleep at the same time. They just dropped, as though all of them were struck by lightning. Oh, my worthy Sebastian, what if ... no, no more ... and yet I think I see it in your face, your destiny. What you should become. Opportunity is knocking for you and in my imagination, I see a crown being placed on your head.

SEBASTIAN
What, are you dreaming?

ANTONIO
Don't you hear what I'm saying?

SEBASTIAN
I do, and it's fantasy talk. Surely, you're talking in your sleep. What is it you said? It's strange for you to be asleep with your eyes wide open like that. You're standing, speaking, moving, yet obviously fast asleep.

ANTONIO

Sebastian, my friend, you're letting your destiny sleep. Or, rather, die. Seize it while you are awake.

SEBASTIAN

What a distinct snore you have. There's meaning in the sound of your snores.

ANTONIO

I'm not usually serious, but right now I'm being completely serious. You also need to be serious, if you follow me to your destiny, though it obviously frightens you.

SEBASTIAN

I am as calm as standing water.

ANTONIO

I'll teach you how to flow.

SEBASTIAN

Do so. To ebb, that is my inherent lazy nature.

ANTONIO

Oh, if you only knew how close to success you are, while you mock my plans. The more you make fun of the plan, the more serious I am about it. 'Ebbing' men wind up at the bottom, sunk by their own fear and laziness.

SEBASTIAN

Go on. I can see it in your eyes and your face that this is truly a serious matter and you're having trouble saying exactly what you want to say.

**ANTONIO**

This is what I'm saying. Although this lord with the poor memory[1], who will be barely remembered after he is dead and buried, almost persuaded – for he is the very spirit of persuasion – the King into believing that his son is alive, though that's as preposterous as saying that the sleeping men here are, in fact, actually swimming.

**SEBASTIAN**

I have no hope that he survived.

**ANTONIO**

Oh, but out of that 'no hope' you have such great hopes! That 'no hope' is such high hope that even the most ambitious could never reach it. Will you agree with me that Ferdinand drowned?

**SEBASTIAN**

He's gone.

**ANTONIO**

Then tell me, who's the next heir to Naples?

**SEBASTIAN**

Claribel.

**ANTONIO**

Her, the new Queen of Tunis, she who lives thirty miles beyond the edge of the world, she who can't even receive a message sent from Naples? Only the Sun itself could deliver her a letter. The Man in the Moon himself is too slow. To send

---

1 Referring to Gonzalo

her a message, it would take the time between the birth of a newborn until he was shaving. Claribel, who caused our shipwreck? It was our destiny to be saved, and it is now our destiny to act. What's past is prologue. The destiny is yours and I am here to help you make it a reality.

SEBASTIAN
What are you talking about? It's true that my brother's daughter is the Queen of Tunis and that she is the heir to Naples. And it's also true that there's a bit of distance between Tunis and Naples. But so what?

ANTONIO
A distance whose every foot seems to cry out, 'How can Claribel travel so far back to Naples? She should stay in Tunis and let Sebastian wake up.' If these sleeping men were really dead, they'd certainly be no worse off than they are now. There are many men who could rule Naples just as well as this sleeping man here, lords that can carry on as vociferously and unnecessarily as Gonzalo. I could do it myself. Oh, if you only had my brain, you'd understand how you are really asleep, blind to this opportunity! Do you understand what I'm telling you?

SEBASTIAN
I think I do.

ANTONIO
And does the good fortune of this present situation make you happy?

**SEBASTIAN**

I remember you taking your power from your brother, Prospero.

**ANTONIO**

True. And look how well I wear the robes of power, far better than before. My brother's servants used to be my equals, now they belong to me.

**SEBASTIAN**

But, for your conscience ...

**ANTONIO**

Yes, sir, but just where is the 'conscience'? If conscience were, say, a chill in my foot, I would put on a slipper, that would be something real and tangible. But conscience ... I don't feel any sensation at all. If there were twenty consciences standing between me and Milan, they would melt away before they could hurt me! Here is your sleeping brother, no better than the dirt he's lying on. If he were as dead as he appears to be – and I could easily make him dead with just three inches of my trusty sword – he wouldn't stand in our way. As for these other men, they'll take to us as a cat takes to a bowl of milk. They'll reset the clock to any time we tell them.

**SEBASTIAN**

My friend, your own story will be my precedent. Just as you took Milan, I'll take Naples. Draw your sword. One stroke will free you of the tribute which you pay and I, the new King of Naples, will love you.

ANTONIO

We draw together. When I raise my hand, you raise yours, too, and we both bring our swords down on Gonzalo.

SEBASTIAN

Wait, just one thing. (They speak quietly together.)

(Re-enter ARIEL, invisible, with music and song.)

ARIEL

My master, through his sorcery, foresees the danger that you, his friend, are in. He has sent me forth to make sure these men stay alive and to keep his plan from dying.
(ARIEL sings in GONZALO's ear)
> While you here do snoring lie,
> Open-eyed conspiracy
> His time does take.
> If of life you have a care,
> Shake off slumber, and beware.
> Awake, awake!¹

ANTONIO

We must act quickly.

GONZALO

(Waking up) Help, everyone, save the King!

(The OTHERS awaken.)

ALONSO

What's going on? Why did you wake all of us? Why are your swords out? Why do you look like that?

---

1 The original rhyme scheme has been retained. In the original Shakespearean rhyme scheme, "conspiracy" is pronounced conspira-sie, rhyming with "lie".

GONZALO
What's the matter?

SEBASTIAN
While we stood here, guarding you while you slept, we heard a monstrous bellowing, like bulls or, rather, lions. Didn't it wake you? It was incredibly loud.

ALONSO
I didn't hear anything.

ANTONIO
Oh, it was a noise that would even scare a monster, that would make the earth shake! It must have been the roar of a whole herd of lions.

ALONSO
Did you hear it, Gonzalo?

GONZALO
It's true, sir, I heard a humming sound, and a strange one at that, and that's what woke me. I shook you, sir, and cried out. As soon as I opened my eyes, I saw their weapons drawn. There was definitely a noise. It's best we be on our guard or that we leave this place altogether. We should draw our weapons.

ALONSO
Lead us out of here and let's continue searching for my poor son.

GONZALO
May God keep him safe from these beasts, since he is surely
on this island!

ALONSO
Lead away.

ARIEL
Prospero, my lord, shall know what I have done;
So, King, go safely on to seek your son.

(All exit.)

# ACT II

SCENE 2: Another part of the island.

(Enter CALIBAN, with a load of wood. Thunder can be heard.)

CALIBAN
I hope that all of the diseases that breed in bogs, marshes and flats infect Prospero, and that he is eaten up by infection, inch by inch! I know his spirits are listening, but I need to curse him anyway. But they can't pinch me, scare me with fright shows, throw me in the mud, nor mislead me unless he orders them to do so. But he sends them to punish me for every little thing, sometimes in the form of apes, grimacing and chattering at me and then biting me. And sometimes he sends them like porcupines for me to step on with my bare feet. Sometimes I am bound by snakes, who hiss at me with their forked tongues until I go mad. (Enter TRINCULO.) Now, look at this! Here comes one of his spirits to torment

me for being too slow in bringing the wood back. I'll hide and maybe he won't see me.

(CALIBAN lies flat on the ground, hiding himself.)

TRINCULO

There are no bushes or shrubs here to shelter myself against the weather, and I can hear another storm coming. Listen to that wind. That huge black cloud over there looks like a filthy tankard, ready to spill out its liquor. If there's a storm like the last one, I don't know where I could protect myself from it. Those clouds will undoubtedly pour down rain by the bucket full. (TRINCULO sees CALIBAN) What have we here? A man or a fish? Dead or alive? A fish. He smells like a fish. It's a very old and fish-like smell, definitely not a fresh fish. What a strange fish! Were I in England now, as I once was, and had even a painting of this fish, not even the most foolish man there would give me even a single piece of silver for it. In England, even this monster would be considered a man. In England, any old monster could be taken for a man. When they will not give a single penny in charity to a lame beggar, they will lay out ten to see a dead Indian. Legs like a man and his fins are like arms! And he's warm! I am changing my mind, this is no fish. This is an islander that must have been struck by lightning. (The sound of thunder is heard.) Oh, the storm is back! My best bet is to crawl under this coat. There's no other shelter around. (TRINCULO crawls under CALIBAN's cloak, his head and torso hidden, but his legs showing, making CALIBAN look like a creature with four legs.) Misery makes for strange bedfellows. I will have to stay here until the storm has passed.

(Enter STEPHANO drunkenly singing, a bottle in his hand.)

STEPHANO

> I shall no more to sea, to sea,
> Here shall I die ashore ...

(STEPHANO stops singing to reflect.)
This is a rotten tune to sing at a man's funeral. Well, here's my comfort. (STEPHANO takes a drink and resumes singing.)

> The master, the swabber, the boatswain, and I,
> The gunner, and his mate,
> Loved Mall, Meg, and Marian, and Margery,
> But none of us cared for Kate;
> For she had a tongue with a tang,
> Would cry to a sailor 'Go hang!'
> She loved not the taste of tar nor of pitch,
> Yet a tailor might scratch her wherever she did itch.
> Then to sea, boys, and let her go hang![1]

(STEPHANO stops singing.)
This is a rotten song, too, but here's my comfort. (He takes another drink.)

CALIBAN
Oh, stop tormenting me!

STEPHANO
What's going on? Are there ghosts here? Are you playing tricks on me, showing me savages and men from India? Ha! I didn't escape drowning to now be afraid of your four legs. It has been said that as proper a man as ever went on four legs

---

1 Note that only minor translational changes have been made in this passage, as Stephano's song is intended to rhyme; the original rhyme scheme has been retained.

cannot make him give ground. And it will be said so again, while Stephano breathes through his nose.[1]

CALIBAN
Oh, how this spirit torments me.

STEPHANO
This is some monster of the island with four legs, who has, I believe, a fever. How the devil did he learn our language? I will give him some relief, since we speak the same language. If I can help him and keep him tame, and get him to Naples, he would be a great present for any emperor.

CALIBAN
Do not torment me, I beg you. I'll bring my wood home faster.

STEPHANO
He's having a fit and speaking nonsense. I'll give him a drink from my bottle. If he's never had wine before, it will certainly end his fit. If I can take him with me and keep him tame, I can sell him. Not for too much, but he'll certainly bring money to whoever owns him, that's for sure.

CALIBAN
You haven't hurt me much yet, but I'm sure you will soon. I can tell by your trembling. You're under Prospero's control.

STEPHANO
(Trying to get CALIBAN to drink from his bottle) Come on, open your mouth. This will help your speech. Open up, this

---

1 Stephano is drunk and rambling.

will stop your shaking, I can tell you that for sure. You don't know who your real friends are. Open your mouth again.

TRINCULO
I recognize that voice. It sounds like ... but he drowned! This must be a devil. Help me!

STEPHANO
Four legs and two voices, what a special monster! His front voice speaks well of his friend, but his rear voice only curses and insults. If it takes all of the wine in my bottle to help him recover, then that's what I'll do. Come on. (CALIBAN drinks more.) Good! Now I'll pour some in your other mouth.

TRINCULO
Stephano!

STEPHANO
Is your other mouth calling me? Oh my God, this is a devil, not a monster! I have to get out of here, I don't want to get mixed up with the devil.

TRINCULO
Stephano! If you are Stephano, touch me and speak to me. It's me, Trinculo. Don't be afraid, it's your good friend, Trinculo.

STEPHANO
If you're Trinculo, then come out of there. I'll pull on that smaller set of legs. If any legs are Trinculo's, it's certainly these. (STEPHANO pulls TRINCULO from under the coat.) You are Trinculo! How did you end up as this monster's shit? Does he shit out Trinculos?

TRINCULO

I thought that he was dead, killed by lightning. But didn't you drown, Stephano? I hope that you are really alive. Is the storm over? I hid under the dead monster's coat out of fear of the storm. Are you really alive, Stephano? Oh, Stephano, two Neapolitans survived!

(TRINCULO grasps STEPHANO and hugs him while turning him.)

STEPHANO
Please, don't spin me like that or I'm going to throw up.

CALIBAN
(As an aside) What beautiful creatures these are, if they're not spirits. He's a great god and he brings heavenly liquor. I will worship him.

STEPHANO
How did you escape? How did you get here? Tell the truth, swear on this bottle, how did you get here? I survived by clinging to a wine barrel the sailors had thrown overboard. Swear by this bottle, which I made from tree bark with my own hands, after I washed ashore.

CALIBAN
I'll swear upon that bottle to be your true subject, as that liquor is holy.

STEPHANO
Here. Swear and tell me how you survived.

TRINCULO
I swam ashore, of course, like a duck. I can swim like a duck, I swear it's true.

STEPHANO
(Passing the bottle) Here, kiss the bible. Though you can swim like a duck, you are built like a goose.

(TRINCULO takes a drink.)

TRINCULO
Oh, that's good, Stephano. Do you have any more of this?

STEPHANO
The whole barrel, man. I hid my wine cellar in a cave by the shore. Hey, monster, how are you feeling now?

CALIBAN
Have you come from heaven?

STEPHANO
From the moon, actually. I used to be the Man in the Moon.

CALIBAN
I have seen you in her, and I adore you. My mistress showed me you and your dog and your bush.

STEPHANO
Come here and swear to that. Kiss this bible. I will fill it up again in a short while. I swear.

(CALIBAN drinks.)

TRINCULO

Now that I can see him in the light, this isn't much of a monster. How could I have been afraid of him? He's so weak! The man in the moon? What a poor, gullible monster. Wow, that was a big gulp you took, monster!

CALIBAN

I'll show you every fertile inch of the island and kiss your feet. I beg you, please be my god.

TRINCULO

In this light, he's quite a treacherous and drunken monster! When his god's asleep he'll steal his bottle.

CALIBAN

I'll kiss your feet. I'll vow to be your loyal subject.

STEPHANO

Alright, then, get down and swear it.

TRINCULO

I'll laugh to death at this poor little dog-headed monster. What a disgusting monster! He disgusts me enough to beat him ...

STEPHANO

Come, kiss.

TRINCULO

Except the poor monster's drunk. What a wretched monster!

CALIBAN

I'll show you the best springs, I'll pluck you berries, I'll fish for you, and gather lots of wood. Curse the tyrant that I serve! I won't fetch him any more wood. Instead, I will follow you, you wondrous man.

TRINCULO

What a ridiculous monster, feeling such wonder about a poor drunk!

CALIBAN

I beg you, let me take you where you can find crabs. With my long nails, I'll dig for nuts and roots for you. I'll find you a bird's nest and show you how to snare the nimble marmoset. I'll bring you to hazelnut clusters, and sometimes I'll even capture young seabirds for you, right off the rocks. Will you go with me?

STEPHANO

I'll go, but please, lead us there without talking. Trinculo, with the King and everyone else drowned, all of this is ours for the taking. Here, take my bottle. Trinculo, my friend, we'll get that filled up again soon enough.

CALIBAN

(Singing drunkenly) Farewell, master. Farewell, farewell!

TRINCULO

A howling monster, a drunken monster!

CALIBAN

No more dams I'll make for fish;
Nor fetch wood for firing
You requiring,
Nor scrape your plates, nor wash your dish.
'Ban 'Ban, Ca-Caliban,
Has a new master, got a new man.[1]
Freedom, high-day!
High-day, freedom!
Freedom, high-day, freedom!


STEPHANO

Oh, brave monster! Lead the way.


(They exit.)

---

1 Caliban's rhyme scheme has been retained

# ACT III

SCENE 1: In front of PROSPERO's chambers.

(Enter FERDINAND, carrying a log.)

FERDINAND
There are some sports that are painful, but it's the strain itself that makes them fun. Some kinds of degradation are done for noble reasons. And you can do poor things that lead to rich results. This hard work would be as loathsome as it is beneath me if I wasn't working for a woman who energizes me and makes my hard work a pleasure. Oh, she is ten times as nice as her father is mean, and he is made out of pure nastiness. I have thousands of these logs to move and make into piles on his strict orders. My beautiful mistress cries when she sees me work and says that such harsh work has never been inflicted on someone like me before this. Her words make me forget my work, her sweet thoughts refresh me as I slave away.

(Enter MIRANDA and PROSPERO, though PROSPERO remains at a distance, unseen.)

MIRANDA

Please, I beg you, don't work so hard. I wish the lightning had burned up those logs that you are piling. Please, set them down and rest. When this burns, it will cry for all the hard work inflicted on you. My father is hard at his studies. Please, rest. He'll be gone for at least three hours.

FERDINAND

My dear mistress, I won't be finished until at least after sunset.

MIRANDA

If you sit down, I'll carry the logs for a while. Please, give me that. I'll carry it to the pile.

FERDINAND

No, my precious, I'd rather strain my muscles and break my back before letting you suffer like this while I sit, lazily watching.

MIRANDA

I can do it just as well as you can. In fact, I can do it easier than you, since I would work with a good attitude, and you simply detest the work.

PROSPERO

(As an aside) Oh, you poor worm, you are infected with love! Anyone can see that.

MIRANDA
You look tired.

FERDINAND
No, noble mistress. Even at night, with you standing by me, it is like a fresh morning. I beg you, just so that I can use it in my prayers, what is your name?

MIRANDA
Miranda. Oh, father, I disobeyed you by telling him that!

FERDINAND
Miranda! The name means 'admired'! You are indeed admired, more than anything in the world! I have seen many beautiful women, and have also many times been enslaved by their sweet words. I have liked several women for their various virtues, but I have never been completely and fully in love. Each one, you see, had some defect in her that spoiled her in some way. But you are perfect, you're without peer. You have been created from the best qualities of every creature!

MIRANDA
I have never met another woman. I can't remember seeing another woman's face, except my own in the mirror. I also haven't seen any men other than you and my dear father. I have no idea what people look like off this island. But I swear by my modesty, the most precious thing I have, I couldn't possibly ever want any other man but you. I can't even imagine another man. Listen to me babbling away. I've forgotten my father's lessons in that regard.

FERDINAND

I am a prince, Miranda. Due to circumstances, I think that I'm now a King, though I wish I weren't. Ordinarily, I wouldn't carry these logs any more than I would let flies breed in my mouth. But I'm speaking from my very soul, the very instant that I saw you, my heart flew into your service. I am your slave. For you, I am a patient log-man.

MIRANDA

Do you love me?

FERDINAND

I want the heavens and the earth to bear witness. Reward me if I'm speaking the truth and strike me dead if I am lying. More than anything else in the world, I love you, I prize you, I honor you.

MIRANDA

(Crying) I'm so foolish to be crying over something that makes me so happy.

PROSPERO

(As an aside) What an encounter between two people so in love! May God bless this growing love between them!

FERDINAND

Why are you crying?

MIRANDA

I'm crying because I'm not worthy to give you what I desire to give you, and even less worthy to take what I'm dying to have. But this is a waste of time. The more I try to hide what I'm feeling, the bigger it grows. (To herself) Oh, stop being so bashful and cunning! Just be straightforward and innocent! (To FERDINAND) If you will marry me, I will be your wife. If not, I will die a virgin, always devoted to you. You can deny me marriage, but I'll be your devoted slave whether you want me to be or not.

FERDINAND
Dearest, I choose you as my wife, and I will be devoted to you forever.

MIRANDA
My husband, then?

FERDINAND
Yes, with my heart bound to you stronger than how a slave wishes for freedom. Take my hand.

MIRANDA
Here's my hand, along with my heart. Goodbye for now, I will see you in half an hour.

FERDINAND
A thousand thousand goodbyes to you!

(Exit FERDINAND and MIRANDA, separately.)

PROSPERO
I can't match the happiness of those two, especially given what a surprise they've had, but I'm as happy as I can be. Now

I must return to my studies. I have much to do with regard to this new development before supper time.

(PROSPERO exits.)

# ACT III

SCENE 2: Another part of the island.

(Enter CALIBAN, STEPHANO and TRINCULO. They have been wandering and drinking.)

STEPHANO
Don't tell me that ... when the barrel runs out, we will drink water, but not a drop of that until we have to. So, drink up. Servant-monster, drink to me.

TRINCULO
Servant-monster! How crazy this island is! They say there are only five people on this island: there's the three of us, and if the other two are as drunk as we are, this island is sure to sink.

STEPHANO
Drink when I tell you to, servant-monster. Your eyes look like they've almost sunk into your head.

TRINCULO

Where else should they be? He would be quite a monster indeed if they had sunk in his tail.

STEPHANO

My man-monster is so drunk that he can't speak anymore. As for me, no liquid can sink me. Not even the sea. I swam, off and on, a hundred and five miles before coming to the shore. Monster, you shall be my lieutenant, or my standard.[1]

TRINCULO

Your lieutenant, if you so desire, but he's certainly not standard.

STEPHANO

We will be brave and never run away in our army, Monsieur Monster.

TRINCULO

Nor are you going to walk away, either. You'll just lie there, silent, like sleeping dogs.

STEPHANO

Monster, please just say one word. A good monster would speak to me.

CALIBAN

How is your highness? Let me lick your shoes. I'll not serve him (points to TRINCULO). He is not brave.

---

1 A standard is a flag bearer. This remains untranslated into modern English in order to set up the pun in the next line.

TRINCULO

You lie, you stupid monster. I'm so in shape, I could beat an officer of the law. You drunk fish, you. Could a true coward drink as much as I did today? Do you tell such monstrous lies because you're half-fish and half-monster?

CALIBAN

Look how he mocks me! Will you let him get away with that, my lord?

TRINCULO

'Lord', he says! What an idiot this monster is!

CALIBAN

Look, he said it again! Bite him to death, I beg you.

STEPHANO

Trinculo, be civil. If you prove yourself disloyal to me, I'll hang you on the next tree we come across! This poor monster is now my subject, and, as such, he will be treated with dignity.

CALIBAN

I thank you, my noble lord. Will you now, please, listen to my earlier request?

STEPHANO

Of course I will. Kneel before me and repeat it. I will stand, as will Trinculo.

(Enter ARIEL, invisible.)

CALIBAN

As I told you before, I am subject to a tyrant, a sorcerer. By his cunning, he has cheated me out of this island.

ARIEL

(Invisible, pretending to be TRINCULO's voice) You lie.

CALIBAN

(To TRINCULO) *You* lie, you silly monkey. I wish my brave master would destroy you. I do not lie.

STEPHANO

Trinculo, if you interrupt him again, I'll knock your teeth out.

TRINCULO

But I didn't say anything.

STEPHANO

Well, then, just be quiet. Proceed.

CALIBAN

As I was saying, he stole this island from me using his magic. If your highness will get revenge on him – and I am certain you are great enough – because I am too scared to ...

STEPHANO

That's for sure.

CALIBAN

You will become lord of this island, and I will faithfully serve you.

STEPHANO
Well, how should we go about doing this? Can you bring me to this man?

CALIBAN
Yes, yes, my lord. I will take you to him when he sleeps and you can pound a nail into his head.

ARIEL
You lie, you cannot.

CALIBAN
What an idiotic fool this man is! You rotten piece of crap! I beg you, your highness, rain down blows on him and take his bottle from him. When that's gone, he'll have nothing to drink but sea water. I won't show him where to find fresh water.

STEPHANO
Trinculo, watch yourself. Interrupt this monster again with just one more word and I'll show you no mercy. I'll make ground fish out of you.

TRINCULO
Why, what did I do? I didn't say anything. I'm getting out of here.

STEPHANO
Didn't you say that he lied?

ARIEL
You lie.

STEPHANO

Oh, do I? Take that. (STEPHANO hits TRINCULO) Want another? Just lie to me one more time.

TRINCULO

I didn't lie to you. I know that you're out of your mind, but are you deaf, too? Curse that bottle of yours! This is what happens when you drink too much. Curse that monster of yours and I hope your hand rots off!

CALIBAN

Ha, ha, ha!

STEPHANO

(To CALIBAN) Now, go on with your story. (To STEPHANO) You are excused to go wait over there (indicating to the side).

CALIBAN

Beat him up. After a while, I'll beat him, too.

STEPHANO

(To TRINCULO) Go farther away. (To CALIBAN) Okay, proceed with your story.

CALIBAN

Okay, as I said, he tends to sleep in the afternoon. That's when you can brain him. You can do it with one of his books, or you can use a log to bash in his skull. Or you can stab him with a stake, or cut his throat with your knife. Remember, first grab his magic books. Without them, he's just a drunk like me. He'll have no spirits to command, since they all hate him as much as I do. Burn the books. He has some great 'home furnishings' – that's what he calls them – that he'll use to decorate his house, when he actually gets one. The most important concern is his beautiful daughter. He himself admits that she has no equal. The only woman I've ever seen was Sycorax, my mother, and she certainly surpasses her. You can't even compare the two.

### STEPHANO
Is she really such a beautiful girl?

### CALIBAN
Yes, lord. I'll bet she'll make a great bride for you, and bear you brave and beautiful children.

### STEPHANO
Monster, I will kill this man. His daughter and I will be King and Queen – God save us! – and Trinculo and you will be our viceroys. How do you like that, Trinculo?

### TRINCULO
Excellent.

### STEPHANO
Give me your hand, I'm sorry I hit you. But, remember, please remain civil.

### CALIBAN
Within half an hour, he will be asleep. Will you destroy him then?

STEPHANO
Yes, on my honor.

ARIEL
I must tell my master this.

CALIBAN
You've made me so happy, I'm full of joy. Let's celebrate.
Will you sing the song you taught me a while ago?

STEPHANO
I'll do anything you ask, monster, within reason. Come on,
Trinculo, let's sing.  (STEPHANO sings)
>    Flout them and scout them,
>    And scout them and flout them;
>    Thought is free.

CALIBAN
That's not the song.

(ARIEL plays a tune on a small drum and pipe.)

STEPHANO
Where's that music coming from?

TRINCULO
That's the song we wanted, played by Nobody.

STEPHANO
(To the invisible source of the music) If you're a man, show
yourself. If you're a devil, then go back to hell.

TRINCULO
Oh, God, forgive my sins!

STEPHANO
Dead men must pay their debts. I challenge you. God help us!

CALIBAN
Are you afraid?

STEPHANO
No, monster, not me.

CALIBAN
Don't be afraid. This island is full of noises: strange sounds and sweet melodies that will make you feel good and which never actually hurt anyone. Sometimes I hear a thousand instruments playing and humming in my ears. Sometimes I hear voices which, if I have just woken from a long sleep, will put me right back to sleep. And then I dream of clouds opening up and showering me with riches. Such dreams that when I wake up, I cry because I want to go back into the dream again.

STEPHANO
This will make a fantastic kingdom for me, where music plays for free.

CALIBAN
Only when Prospero is dead.

STEPHANO
That will happen soon enough. I know the plan.

TRINCULO

The music is fading away. Let's follow it, and then get on with the plan after that.

STEPHANO

Lead us, monster. We'll follow you. I wish I could see this invisible drummer. He plays really well.

TRINCULO

Are you coming, monster? I'm right behind you, Stephano.

(They exit.)

# ACT III

SCENE 3: Another part of the island.

(Enter ALONSO, SEBASTIAN, ANTONIO, GONZALO, ADRIAN, FRANCISCO and OTHERS.)

GONZALO
I swear, I can't go any further, sir. My old bones ache. We're wandering through a maze here, going this way and that. If you don't mind, I need to rest.

ALONSO
Old man, I can't blame you. I'm so weary that I feel it all the way down to my soul. Sit down and rest. With all we've been through, I'm losing hope. The man we're looking for is drowned and the ocean mocks us more and more the farther we go on land. We should just let him go.

ANTONIO
(Aside to SEBASTIAN) I'm glad that he's lost hope. Don't back out of our plan just yet.

SEBASTIAN
(Aside to ANTONIO) We just need to wait until the time is right.

ANTONIO
(Aside to SEBASTIAN) Let's make it tonight. They're exhausted from our travels. They're not even close to being as vigilant as they ordinarily would be.

SEBASTIAN
(Aside to ANTONIO) I agree, tonight. That should be all we say for now about this.

(Solemn and strange music plays. PROSPERO enters from above, invisible. Enter several strange SPIRITS, bringing in a banquet and dancing around it with gentle gestures of greeting, inviting all to come and eat. They then depart.)

ALONSO
Do you hear that music? My friends, listen!

GONZALO
Marvelous sweet music!

ALONSO
Heaven help us! What were those things?

SEBASTIAN
A living puppet show. Now I'll believe that unicorns exist and that, in Arabia, there is a tree that's the throne of the phoenix, and that he's ruling there right now.

ANTONIO
I'll believe both along with anything else you tell me. Just

come to me, saying anything, and I'll swear it's true. Travelers never lie, no matter what the fools at home accuse them of.

GONZALO
If I was in Naples and told them about this, would they believe me? If I were to say that I saw islanders such as these – and, surely, these are the people of this island – who, though shaped like monsters, are more polite and more kind than any human being, would anyone believe me? Anyone at all?

PROSPERO
(As an aside) Good lord, you're absolutely right. Some of you are worse than devils, that's for sure.

ALONSO
I can't stop being amazed by these strange spirits, their gestures and their sounds. Even though they did not speak, it was an incredible kind of silent language.

PROSPERO
(As an aside) Time for me to go.

FRANCISCO
They vanished so strangely.

SEBASTIAN
It doesn't matter. They left the food behind and we're all certainly hungry. Wouldn't you like to taste some of this?

ALONSO
Not me.

GONZALO

Have faith, sir, there's nothing to be afraid of. When we were boys, who would have believed there were mountain people with dewlaps like bulls, whose throats had hanging folds of skin? Or that there were men with heads in their chests? These days, travelers regularly report such things.

ALONSO

Alright, I'll eat, even though this might be my last meal. It's okay, since I think the best is behind me. Brother, my Duke, please eat with us.

(Thunder and lightning. Enter ARIEL, in the form of a harpy. ARIEL claps his wings upon the table and, via some stage mechanism, the banquet vanishes.)

ARIEL

(To ALONSO, ANTONIO and SEBASTIAN) You three are men of sin, whom Destiny made the sea belch you up onto this island. This island which does not support life, and you men are here because you are unfit to live. I have made you crazy, and even brave men who are driven crazy can be forced to hang or drown themselves. (ALONSO, SEBASTIAN, etc., draw their swords) You fools! My fellow harpies and I carry out the orders of Fate. Your swords are useless against us. You might as well try to fight the wind or water with them. If you try to remove one feather from my body, the result would be the same. We are invulnerable. Even if you had the power to hurt us, your swords now weigh far too much for you to even lift them. But remember – and it's my job to remind you – that the three of you from Milan stole Prospero's Duke-dom, casting him out to sea, and that same sea has now tak-en revenge on you in the name of Prospero and his innocent daughter. For your foul deeds, the gods have upset the land and the sea, creating the tempest that brought you here, and setting all creatures of the Earth against you. They've taken your son, Alonso, and commanded me to punish you, a slow torture worse than death. My punishment will be with you every step of the way from now on. The only way to protect yourselves against the gods – who are ready to punish you on this lonely island – is for you to be sincerely sorry in your hearts for what you have done, and to begin living good clean lives from now on.

(ARIEL vanishes in thunder. The SPIRITS enter again, to soft music, and dance, with mocking gestures and grimaces. They carry out the table.)

PROSPERO
You have played the role of a harpy well, my Ariel. You were both fierce and graceful. You followed my instructions regarding your speech perfectly. In the same lifelike way, and also following instructions perfectly, my other servants also performed well. My magic is working, and my enemies are now consumed with their perceived predicament. They are now under my power, and I'll leave them in their present state of confusion while I visit young Ferdinand, whom they think has drowned, and his, and my own, beloved darling.

(PROSPERO exits.)

GONZALO
For the love of God, sir, why are you frozen, staring like that?

ALONSO
Oh, it's horrible, horrible! I thought the clouds were speaking to me, the wind and the thunder, like a low and eerie organ, saying the name 'Prospero', reciting my crimes, telling me that this is why my son has drowned. I want to join him in the sea, sinking lower than any anchor has ever sunk. I want to lie there with him in the mud.

(ALONSO exits.)

SEBASTIAN
I'll fight these devils, one at a time if I have to.

ANTONIO
I've got your back.

(Exit SEBASTIAN and ANTONIO.)

GONZALO
The three of them are desperate. Their great guilt is eating away at them like a slow-acting poison. Those of you who are young and fit, please, follow them and keep them from hurting themselves in their mad mission.

ADRIAN
Follow them, please.

(All exit.)

# ACT IV

SCENE 1: In front of PROSPERO's chambers.

(Enter PROSPERO, FERDINAND and MIRANDA.)

PROSPERO
(To FERDINAND) If I have punished you too harshly, your compensation more than makes up for it. I'm giving you a third of my own life, the very thing I live for. You may have her hand. All of the labors I put you through were tests of your love, and you passed my test with flying colors. As God is my witness, I give you her hand. Oh, Ferdinand! Don't laugh at how I brag about her. You will soon see that she is far beyond any praise that could ever be given to her.

FERDINAND
I would believe that even if an oracle told me differently.

PROSPERO
Then, as my gift, as well as something you have earned on

your own, take my daughter. But if you take her virginity before the wedding takes place, know that your marriage will *not* be blessed. Rather, your marriage will be filled with hate, contempt and discord. Your marriage bed will be cursed and poisoned to such a degree that you will both hate it. So, be careful for now, and bask in Hymen, the marriage god's, light.

FERDINAND

Given how much I hope for a peaceful life, great children and a long life filled with love, I will not allow myself to be tempted by my lust, not in the darkest bedroom, the most opportune place or the strongest seduction. Nothing can take away the sweet anticipation of what we will experience on our wedding night. On the day of celebration, my mind will surely be so consumed with thoughts of the coming night that it will feel like Phoebus, the sun god's, chariot horses had gone lame, or that the night itself had been bound up, chained just below the horizon.

PROSPERO

Very well said. Sit, then, and talk with her. She's now yours. Come, Ariel! My hard-working servant, Ariel!

(Enter ARIEL.)

ARIEL

What do you need, my powerful master? I'm here.

PROSPERO

You and your fellow spirits performed your duties well, and now I have another trick for you to perform. Go and bring that rabble here. I give you power over them. Incite them into the need to act quickly. I want to give this young couple here a glimpse of my magic. I have promised them a good show and now they expect one.

ARIEL
Right now?

PROSPERO
Yes, right away.

ARIEL
> Before you can say 'come' and 'go',
> And breathe twice, and cry 'so, so',
> Each one, tripping on his toe,
> Will be here with mop and mow.
> Do you love me, master? No?[1]

PROSPERO
Go, my dear Ariel. Do not come back until you hear me call for you.

ARIEL
I understand.

(ARIEL exits.)

PROSPERO
(To FERDINAND) I'm trusting you to be honorable. Don't give in to your desires. Words only go so far when compared

---

1 The original rhyme scheme has been retained.

with the fire in your blood. Exercise maximum restraint, lest you break your vow!

FERDINAND
I assure you, sir, the pure snow of my heart is enough to quench the burning heat of my loins.

PROSPERO
Good! Now come, Ariel, bring a servant with you. We may need extra help. Now, come quickly. Silence! Eyes front! Shh, be silent.
(Soft music plays.)

(Enter IRIS.)

IRIS
        Ceres, most generous lady, your rich leas
        Of wheat, rye, barley, beans, oats, and peas;
        Your grassy mountains, where live nibbling sheep,
        And flat meadows thatched with corn, them to
    keep;
        Your banks abounding in marsh marigolds and
    woven brims,
        Which spongy April at your request betrims,
        To make cold nymphs chaste crowns; and your
    broom groves,
        Whose shadow the dismissed bachelor loves,
        Being without lass; your pole-clipped vineyard;
        And your sea shore, sterile and rocky hard,
        Where you yourself do air – the Queen of the sky,
        Whose watery arch and messenger am I,

Bids you leave these; and with her sovereign grace,

Here on this grass plot, in this very place,

To come and sport. Her peacocks fly amain.

(JUNO descends in her chariot.)

Approach, rich Ceres, her to entertain.[1]

(Enter CERES.)

CERES

Hail, many-colored messenger, that never

Do disobey the wife of Jupiter;

Who, with your saffron wings, upon my flowers

Diffuse honey drops, refreshing showers;

And with each end of your blue bow do crown

My shaded acres and my unshrubbed down,

Rich scarf to my proud earth – why has your Queen

Summoned me to this place, to this short-grassed green?

IRIS

A contract of true love to celebrate,

And some donation freely to estate

On the blessed lovers.

CERES

Tell me, heavenly bow,

---

1 Note that only minor translational changes have been made in this poem, as Iris' lines are intended to rhyme; the original rhyme scheme has been retained. The same goes for the following lines of Iris, Ceres and Juno, who speak and sing in rhymes. Iris, Ceres and Juno are Prospero's spirits, masquerading as classical goddesses. Ceres is played by Ariel, as noted in the dialogue below but not described in Shakespeare's original stage directions.

> If Venus or her son, as you do know,
> Do now attend the Queen? Since they did plot
> The means that dusky Dis my daughter got,
> Her and her blind boy's scandaled company
> I have forsworn.

IRIS

> Of her society
> Be not afraid. I met her Deity
> Cutting the clouds towards Paphos, and her son
> Dove-drawn with her. Here thought they to have done
> Some wanton charm upon this man and maid,
> Whose vows are that no bed ritual shall be paid
> Until Hymen's torch be lighted; but in vain.
> Mars's hot minion is returned again;
> Her waspish-headed son has broken his arrows,
> Swears he will shoot no more, but play with sparrows,
> And be a boy right out.

(JUNO comes down to the stage.)

CERES

Highest Queen of State,
Great Juno, comes; I know her by her gait.

JUNO

How is my generous sister? Go with me
To bless this couple, that they may prosperous be,
And honored in their issue.

(JUNO and CERES sing.)

JUNO

> Honor, riches, marriage-blessing,
> Long continuance, and increasing,
> Hourly joys be still upon you!
> Juno sings her blessings on you.

CERES

> Earth's increase, abundance plenty,
> Barns and silos never empty;
> Vines with clustering bunches growing,
> Plants with abundant burden bowing;
> Spring come to you at the farthest,
> In the very end of harvest!
> Scarcity and want shall shun you,
> Ceres' blessing so is on you.

FERDINAND

This is a most majestic vision, harmonious and charming. Are these spirits?

PROSPERO

Yes, spirits. I have called them here with my magic to entertain us.

FERDINAND

I want to live here forever. How unique and wise my new father-in-law is, making this place a true paradise.

(JUNO and CERES whisper with one another and then send IRIS on a mission.)

PROSPERO
Now, quiet. Juno and Ceres are whispering about something serious. There's something else to be done. Be quiet or the spell will be broken.

IRIS
>You nymphs, called Naiads, of the winding brooks,
>With your crowns made of grass and ever harmless looks,
>Leave your streams, and on this green land
>Answer your summons; Juno does command.
>Come, temperate nymphs, and help to celebrate
>A contract of true love; be not too late.
>(Enter several NYMPHS.)
>You sun burned field workers, of August weary,
>Come to this place from your trenches, and be merry;
>Make holiday; your rye straw hats put on,
>And these fresh nymphs encounter every one
>In country footing.

(Enter REAPERS (i.e., field workers), dressed appropriately. They join in with the NYMPHS in a graceful dance. As with the goddesses, the REAPERS and NYMPHS are really PROSPERO's SPIRITS, masquerading as specific characters. Toward the end of the dance, PROSPERO is suddenly startled and speaks.)

PROSPERO

(As an aside) I just remembered that that beast Caliban and his confederates are conspiring to kill me. The time is almost here. (To the SPIRITS) Well done. Now, no more!

(A strange, hollow and confused noise is heard, and all supernatural beings vanish.)

FERDINAND

That's strange. Your father is suddenly really agitated.

MIRANDA

I've never seen him so upset before.

PROSPERO

(To FERDINAND) You look like something is bothering you, as though you are suddenly concerned about something. Cheer up. The celebration is now at an end. The beings you saw were all spirits, and have now melted away into thin air. And just like this insubstantial vision, everything – the towers topped with clouds, the gorgeous palaces, the solemn temples, the great globe itself – everything in the world will eventually dissolve away. Just like this little pageant that faded away, everything else will also fade, leaving no trace. We are such stuff as dreams are made on, and our little life ends with sleep. My boy, I am a bit upset, bear with me. My old brain is troubled. Don't be disturbed by my infirmity. If you wish, go to my chambers and rest. I'll go for a short walk to calm my feverish mind.

FERDINAND and MIRANDA

We hope you feel better.

(FERDINAND and MIRANDA exit.)

PROSPERO
Come here, Ariel. I summon you with my thoughts. Come.

(Enter ARIEL.)

ARIEL
I obey your thoughts. What do you need me to do?

PROSPERO
Spirit, we must prepare to meet with Caliban.

ARIEL
Yes, my commander. When I was playing Ceres, I wanted to remind you of it, but I was afraid that it might anger you.

PROSPERO
Tell me again, where did you leave those lowlifes?

ARIEL
As I told you before, sir, they were all fired up from drinking, so full of valor that they struck out at the wind for blowing in their faces, they beat the ground for kissing their feet, but always keeping their plan in mind. Then I beat my small drum which caused them to prick up their ears, like untamed colts, open their eyes, and lift up their noses, as though they could smell the music. They were so under my spell that, like calves, they followed me through briers, sharp shrubs, stickers and thorns, getting their ankles all cut up. Finally, I left

them in that smelly pond outside your chambers, with that stinky water covering them up to their chins.

PROSPERO
You have done well, my bird. Stay invisible for now. Bring out my fine clothes. I'll use them to catch these thieves.

ARIEL
I'm going, I'm going.

(ARIEL exits.)

PROSPERO
He's a devil, a born devil, on whose nature nurture can never stick. My punishments, no matter how humane, are completely lost on him. He just grows uglier the older he gets, his mind rotting away, on and on. I will torture them all until they roar with pain. (ARIEL re-enters, carrying glittering apparel, etc.) Over here, hang them on this clothes line.

(PROSPERO and ARIEL remain invisible as CALIBAN, STEPHANO and TRINCULO enter, all wet.)

CALIBAN
Please, walk quietly. Not even a blind mole should be able to hear our footsteps. We are now near his chambers.

STEPHANO
Monster, your spirit, which you say is harmless, has done little more than play pranks on us.

TRINCULO

Monster, I smell like horse piss, which is making my nose quite upset.

STEPHANO

Mine, too. Did you hear that, monster? If I become angry with you, you'd better watch out ...

TRINCULO

You were just a poor lost monster.

CALIBAN

Please, lord, keep your faith in me. Be patient. The prize awaiting us will make up for our recent indignity. Now please be quiet. It's as silent as midnight here.

TRINCULO

Yes, but to lose our bottle in the pond!

STEPHANO

There is not only disgrace and dishonor in that, monster, but infinite loss.

TRINCULO

That's far more upsetting to me than just getting wet. Yet you called this spirit 'harmless', monster.

STEPHANO

No matter what it takes, I'll get my bottle back.

CALIBAN

I beg you, my king, be quiet. Right here, this is the door to his chambers. We must be silent as we enter. Please, do what must be done to make this island your own forever. Do this and I, your Caliban, will be your worshipping foot-licker.

STEPHANO
Give me your hand. I'm beginning to feel dangerous.

TRINCULO
Oh, King Stephano! Oh, my friend! Oh worthy Stephano! Look at this wardrobe laid out for you!

CALIBAN
Leave it alone, you fool. It's just trash.

TRINCULO
No, monster; we know nice clothing when we see it. (Trying on a robe) Oh, King Stephano!

STEPHANO
Take off that robe, Trinculo. It's obviously meant for me.

TRINCULO
Your Grace shall have it.

CALIBAN
To hell with this fool! Why are you going crazy for these old clothes? Leave that alone for now. Let's get back to murder. If he wakes up, he'll pinch us all over, from head to toe, and transform us into something truly strange.

STEPHANO
Be quiet, monster. (To the clothes line) Mistress line, this is my jacket, is it not? Now, is the jerkin under the line? Now,

jerkin, you are likely to lose your hair, and become a bald
jerkin.[1]

TRINCULO

Go ahead and take it. We'll steal with great care, if you so
desire, your Grace.

STEPHANO

That was a good joke, thanks. Here, have this item of clothing as a reward for it. Wit will never go unrewarded when I
am King of this country. 'Steal with great care' is a really great
line. Here, have another piece of clothing.

TRINCULO

Monster, come over here. Put some glue on your fingers and
carry the rest of these clothes with your sticky hands.

CALIBAN

I'm not going to help you with that. Our window is closing
and we're all going to be turned into barnacles or apes with
low foreheads.

STEPHANO

Monster, use your fingers, help us carry this to where I've
hidden my wine barrel. If you don't help us, I'll banish you
from my kingdom. Come on, carry this.

---

1 Translation here has been minimal, as there is a great deal of debate about exactly
what this pun means. Some have suggested that this is an elaborate pun about
the jerkin (a shirt or jacket) being like a sailor who goes to the tropics and contracts a sexually transmitted disease. Others suggest that this pun refers to the
theory, at the time, that one would lose his hair in a hot climate, coupled with
the clothes line resembling, or being made from, hair. Still others have suggested
that this is a dirty joke, with "jerkin" having a masturbatory meaning and ref-
erencing the theory, at the time, that masturbation would make a man go bald.
One translation for this sentence could be: "Now, jacket, you are likely to lose
your hair and become a bald jacket for being underneath there."

TRINCULO
And this.

STEPHANO
Yes, and this.

(A noise of hunters is heard. Enter diverse SPIRITS, in the shape of dogs and hounds, chasing them around. PROSPERO and ARIEL follow, urging the SPIRITS on.)

PROSPERO
Hey, Mountain, hey!

ARIEL
Silver! There they go, Silver!

PROSPERO
Fury, Fury! There, Tyrant, there! Listen, listen! (CALIBAN, STEPHANO and TRINCULO are driven out) (To ARIEL) Go enlist my goblins to make their joints ache, to cramp their muscles, and pinch them all over so that their bruises make them spotted like leopards.

ARIEL
Listen, they're howling.

PROSPERO
Hunt them down. Now, my enemies are all at my mercy. Soon, my work will be done, and you will finally be free. I need you just a little bit longer.

(They exit.)

# ACT V

SCENE 1: In front of PROSPERO'S chambers.

(Enter PROSPERO, in his magic robes, and ARIEL.)

PROSPERO
My plans are finally reaching their conclusion. My magic spells are working well, my spirits obey me, and everything is moving according to schedule. Now, what time is it?

ARIEL
It's six o'clock. My lord, you said we should stop around now.

PROSPERO
Yes, I did say that, back when I raised the tempest. Tell me, my spirit, how are the King and his followers doing?

ARIEL

They are all confined together, just as you ordered. They are all imprisoned in the grove of linden trees that protects your chambers from bad weather. They can't move until you release them. The King, his brother and your own, are all in a somewhat confused state, and the rest are grieving over them, a mix of sorrow and dismay. The one that you called 'the good old lord, Gonzalo' has tears running down his face, into his beard, like dew drops. The magic you cast on them is so strong that if you were to actually see them right now, your heart might even begin to break.

PROSPERO

Do you really think so, spirit?

ARIEL

Mine would, sir, if I were human.

PROSPERO

Then I'm sure mine will. You are a spirit, your touch and feelings are made from air. If you are touched by their present condition, won't I, one of their own, be even more moved? Though I am still infuriated by what they did to, and against, me, I must follow my nobler instincts and seek virtue rather than vengeance. Now that they have been punished and are sorry for their actions, I can end it here. Go release them, Ariel. I will break the spell and restore their sanity. They will be back to themselves soon enough.

ARIEL

I'll go get them, sir.
(ARIEL exits.)

PROSPERO
(Drawing a circle on the ground with his staff)
I have dimmed the noon sun, called forth mutinous winds, and set war between the green land and the green sea. I have done this with your aid, as weak you may be, all of you elves of the hills, brooks, standing lakes and groves. And with you who leave no footprints on the sand as you chase the ebbing Neptune, and who run away when he comes back. And with you half-puppets that make toadstools by the moonlight, you whom the ewe does not bite, and you who make midnight mushrooms late at night. I have given fire to the dread rattling thunder and burned down Jupiter's proud oak with his own lightning bolts. I have caused the cliffs to shake and have uprooted pines and cedars. At my command, the graves have opened, their sleepers awakened and set forth. This is how powerful my magic is. But I give up my black magic now. When I have finished summoning some heavenly music to cast a spell, as I am now doing, I will break my staff and bury it miles beneath the earth, and I will drown my magic book beneath the sea, deeper than any anchor ever sank.

(Solemn music plays. ARIEL enters, and then ALONSO, who is frantically gesturing, followed by GONZALO, SEBASTIAN and ANTONIO, who are similarly gesturing. They are followed by ADRIAN and FRANCISCO. They all enter the circle made by PROSPERO, and stand there, under a spell.)

(PROSPERO watches this and then continues speaking.)
Let this solemn music calm and soothe you, returning your minds to you as they were. Stand there for now, as you are frozen in my spell. Blessed Gonzalo, honorable man, my eyes

cry for you, as I feel for you what you must now be feeling. (As an aside) The spell is dissolving slowly, melting away as the night dissolves into morning. When dawn comes, they should be fully returned to their senses. (To GONZALO) Oh, Gonzalo, you are my savior and loyal to whomever you follow! I will reward you fully, both with words and actions. (To ALONSO) Alonso, you were so cruel in the way you used both me and my daughter. And your brother aided you in this. (To SEBASTIAN) And now you are paying the price for it, Sebastian. (To ANTONIO) You, my brother, my own flesh and blood, you who were so ambitious by nature, who felt no remorse, you who, along with Sebastian, were ready to kill your King. Your inner torment has been the worst ... but I forgive you, as rotten as you may be. (As an aside) They are just beginning to understand what has happened. Soon, the approaching tide will fill in their barren shores, which are still somewhat foul and muddy. Not one of them, not just yet, recognizes me. (To ARIEL) Ariel, bring me my hat and my sword from my chambers. (Exit ARIEL) I will take off these robes and dress as I used to in Milan. Soon, my spirit, you will be free.

(ARIEL returns and sings as he aids PROSPERO in getting dressed.)

ARIEL
Where the bee drinks, there drink I;
In a cowslip flower I lie;
There I sleep when owls do cry.
On the bat's back I do fly
After summer merrily.

Merrily, merrily shall I live now
Under the blossom that hangs on the bough.

PROSPERO
Ah, that's my wonderful Ariel! I will miss you, but, as I promised, you will soon go free. So, so, so. Now, you must go to the King's ship, remaining invisible, and there you will find all of the sailors, asleep, below decks. Find the shipmaster and the boatswain, they should be awake, and bring them here. Please, go now.

ARIEL
I will fly like the wind and be back in less than two heartbeats.

(ARIEL exits.)

GONZALO
This island is full of torment and danger, but also wonder and amazement. God, guide us away from this wild place!

PROSPERO
(To ALONSO) Behold, Your Majesty, it is I, the wronged Duke of Milan, Prospero. To prove I'm real, let me hug you. And to you and your associates, I bid you a hearty welcome.

(PROSPERO grasps ALONSO.)

ALONSO
Whether you are really Prospero or some magic trick designed to punish me even further, as has been the case up to

now, I'm not sure. I can feel your pulse, like a real flesh and blood person, and my sanity has been returning ever since I first saw you. There must be an explanation for this ... if this is really happening. I surrender your dukedom to you and beg your forgiveness. But, please, tell me how you are still alive. And how are you here, on this island?

PROSPERO
(To GONZALO) First, my good friend, let me embrace you, you of limitless honor.

GONZALO
I cannot say if this is real or not.

PROSPERO
You are still feeling some of the subtle magic of the island. It's only natural to still be uncertain about some things. Welcome, all of you, welcome, my friends! (Aside to SEBASTIAN and ANTONIO) But keep in mind, my lords, if I so desired I could easily report you to the King as the traitors you truly are. I know what you have been plotting. But, for now, I'll just keep that under my hat.

SEBASTIAN
(As an aside) It's the devil speaking through him.

PROSPERO
No. I simply choose to forgive you. You, who are so evil that just calling you 'brother' would give me an infection in my mouth. I forgive your worst sin ... all of your sins. But, now I must have my dukedom back from you. You have no real choice in the matter.

ALONSO

If you really are Prospero, tell us how you managed to sur-
vive. How are you here, right now, meeting with us? Just
three hours ago, we shipwrecked here. Oh, the wreck! How
painful it still is! I lost my dear son, Ferdinand.

PROSPERO

I'm sorry for your loss, sir.

ALONSO

I will never get over his death. No amount of time or patience will heal this wound.

PROSPERO

I don't think you have really tried to be patient. Patience has
done wonders for me, and I suffered a loss similar to yours.

ALONSO

You suffered a loss like mine?

PROSPERO

Yes, just as great a loss and just as recent. And I have far
fewer friends to comfort me than you do, as it was my daughter I lost.

ALONSO

A daughter! Oh God, I wish they were both alive, together,
the King and Queen of Naples! I would gladly give my life for
my son, taking his place on the bottom of the ocean floor.
When did you lose your daughter?

PROSPERO

In this last tempest. I see these lords around us are so aston-
ished that they've lost their sense of reason and can hardly believe what they see with their own eyes. But, despite your remaining confusion, please be assured that I am Prospero, the
same duke who was banished from Milan. Having been cast
out, I found myself on the shores of this very island, where you
were shipwrecked, and became master of it. Let's stop there,
as this story will take days to tell;, it's not just some simple
story to be told over breakfast, and certainly not appropriate
for a first meeting. (To ALONSO) Welcome, sir. These chambers are my own royal court. I have only a few servants and
no subjects outside of this room. Please, have a look. As you
have given me my dukedom again, I have something to repay
you with, something just as good. At the very least, you will
be happily surprised, and find the same contentment that the
return of my dukedom brings to me.

(PROSPERO draws back a curtain to reveal FERDINAND
and MIRANDA playing chess.)

MIRANDA
(To FERDINAND) My darling, I think you're cheating.

FERDINAND
No, my dearest love, I wouldn't cheat you for the whole
world.

MIRANDA
Not for the whole world, but for just twenty kingdoms?

I think you would. But, my dear, I would gladly let you get away with it.

ALONSO
If this is just one of the island's illusions, I will have lost my son twice.

SEBASTIAN
Oh, what a miracle!

FERDINAND
(To ALONSO) The sea may be powerful and threatening at times, but it can also be merciful. It looks like I was hasty in cursing it.

(FERDINAND kneels before ALONSO.)

ALONSO
Oh, my son, there is no more love and praise that could possibly be given by his father to his son. Please, get up and tell me how you survived and made it here.

MIRANDA
How wonderful! So many people are here! How beautiful mankind is! Oh, brave new world that has such people in it!

PROSPERO
It's all so new to you.

ALONSO
Who is this girl you're playing with? You can't have known

her for more than three hours. Is she the goddess who first
tore us apart and then brought us back together?

FERDINAND

No, sir, she's quite mortal. But by immortal Providence, she
is mine. I chose her as mine when my father wasn't available
to give me his advice ... I thought I had no father anymore. She
is the daughter of this famous Duke of Milan, whom I have
heard so much about but never saw before. He has given me
a new life, and, by marriage to her, he has also provided me
with a new father.

ALONSO

And I am also a new father, her new father. How strange
it must sound that I must ask my own child for forgiveness!

PROSPERO

No, stop. There's no reason to burden ourselves with what
is past. That's behind us now.

GONZALO

I would have said the same thing, if only I hadn't been so
choked up. Gods above, bless this couple. It is you who paved
the way for all of us to come together here.

ALONSO

Amen to that, Gonzalo!

GONZALO

Was the Duke banished from Milan so that his descendants

could eventually become the Kings of Naples? Oh, this is such an extraordinary thing, one to be written about in gold on eternal pillars. All within the span of one voyage, Claribel married her new husband in Tunis, Ferdinand, her brother, found himself a wife where he was shipwrecked, Prospero regained his dukedom from a barren island, and the rest of us first lost ourselves and then found ourselves again.

ALONSO

(To FERDINAND and MIRANDA) Give me your hands. May anyone who does not wish you happiness be consumed with grief and sorrow.

GONZALO

Amen! (Re-enter ARIEL with the MASTER and BOAT-SWAIN, each looking about with amazement.) Oh look, sir, look! More of us are here! I predicted that that one would never drown, as long as there were still gallows on land. (To BOATSWAIN) You defiled our ship with your blasphemies and foul language. How about now? You have nothing to say now that you're on land? Any news?

BOATSWAIN

The best news is that we have safely found our King and his company. The next best is our ship – which we thought ruined just three hours ago – is ship shape and ready. She's as rigged and ready as when we first set sail.

ARIEL

(Aside to PROSPERO) I took care of it all on my last trip.

PROSPERO
(Aside to ARIEL) My mischievous little spirit!

ALONSO
This is not normal. Things are moving from strange to even stranger. Tell me, how did you get here?

BOATSWAIN
If I was sure that I was awake, I'd certainly try to tell you. We were sleeping like the dead and, somehow, we don't know how, we were all asleep below deck when we heard all sorts of strange noises: roaring, shrieking, howling, jangling chains ... all kinds of sounds, all of them horrible. This woke us up, freeing us from our deathlike sleep, and we saw our grand ship, back in perfect condition, safe and sound. The captain was dancing with joy at the sight. And then, in just an instant, we were separated from the rest, as if in a dream, and brought here under some kind of spell.

ARIEL
(Aside to PROSPERO) Did I do well?

PROSPERO
(Aside to ARIEL) Perfectly, my good worker. You have gained your freedom.

ALONSO
This is a stranger maze than any man has ever gone through before. And these are hardly natural matters. We need an oracle to explain all of this to us.

PROSPERO

Sir, Your Highness, don't trouble yourself trying to figure this all out at once. In time, and it will be sooner rather than later, it will all be explained. My explanation will make all of these events seem far more probable. Until then, just be happy and think about all of the wonderful things you've seen. (Aside to ARIEL) Come over here, spirit. Release Caliban and his companions. Undo the binding spell. (ARIEL exits) How are you doing, my lord? You're still missing a couple of your men, just a couple of strays you've probably forgotten about.

(Re-enter ARIEL, leading in CALIBAN, STEPHANO and TRINCULO, wearing their stolen clothing, looking somewhat ridiculous and still a bit drunk.)

STEPHANO

Each man is responsible for his fellow man, we must all watch each other's backs, because everything is just simple chance. Courage. Courage, our beloved monster!

TRINCULO

If my eyes are not lying to me, what a sight this is.

CALIBAN

Oh Setebos, what handsome spirits these are! How great my master is! I'm afraid that he will punish me.

SEBASTIAN

Ha, ha! What are these things, Antonio, my lord? Can you buy them with money?

ANTONIO

Most likely. There's definitely a market for that one that looks like a fish.

PROSPERO

Take a look at the uniforms on these men, my lords, and then tell me just who they are. As for this misshapen beast, his mother was a witch. She was such a strong witch that she could control the moon and the tides. She shared in the moon's power and was beyond even its control. These three stole from me, and this half-devil bastard conspired with them to murder me in my sleep. Two of these men are yours, and I must admit that this thing of darkness is mine.

CALIBAN

I will be pinched to death.

ALONSO

Wait, isn't this Stephano, my drunken butler?

SEBASTIAN

He's certainly drunk right now. Where did he get wine?

ALONSO

And Trinculo is also stumbling drunk. Where could they have found this liquor that put them in such a state? How did you three get so pickled?

TRINCULO

I have been in such a pickle since I last saw you that I'm worried I'll never be sober again. At least, being this pickled, my body will never decay.

SEBASTIAN
And how are you feeling, Stephano?

STEPHANO
Please don't touch me. I'm not Stephano, rather I'm a walking headache.

PROSPERO
So, you wanted to be king of the island, sir?

STEPHANO
I would have been a sore one at that.

ALONSO
(Pointing to CALIBAN) This is as strange a thing as I've ever seen.

PROSPERO
He is as disproportioned in his manners as he is in his shape. (To CALBIAN) Go, Caliban, to my chambers and take your companions with you. If you want to be forgiven, go clean up the place. I want it spic and span.
CALIBAN
Yes, sir, I will indeed. And from here on, I will be obedient to you. What a jackass I was to mistake this drunkard for a god. I worshipped this dull fool!

PROSPERO
Get to it!

ALONSO

(To STEPHANO and TRINCULO) Go, put that clothing back where you found it.

SEBASTIAN
Or stole it, rather.

(Exit CALIBAN, STEPHANO and TRINCULO.)

PROSPERO
Sir, I invite your Highness and your men into my chambers, where you may rest for the night. We can take the opportunity to spend the evening – part of it, at least – telling stories. I will tell you the story of my life and, particularly, my adventures since I came to this island. In the morning, I will bring you back to your ship and we can leave for Naples, where I hope to witness the marriage of these two lovebirds. And then it's back to Milan for me, where every third thought will be of my own death.

ALONSO
I look forward to hearing the story of your life. It sounds like it's been quite interesting.

PROSPERO
I'll tell you everything, and I promise you calm seas and favorable winds. We will sail so fast that we will catch up with your royal fleet. (Aside to ARIEL) My Ariel, my friend, that is your last job. Then you may be free as the wind. Go, be free and I wish you well. (To all) Please, everyone follow me.

(All exit.)

# EPILOGUE

PROSPERO

> Now my spells are all overthrown,
> And what strength I have is my own,
> Which is most weak. Now it is true,
> I must be here confined by you,
> Or sent to Naples. Let me not,
> Since I have my dukedom got,
> And forgiven the deceiver, dwell
> In this deserted island by your spell;
> But release me from my bands
> With the help of your good hands.
> Gentle breath of yours my sails
> Must fill, or else my project fails,
> Which was to please. Now I want
> Spirits to enforce, magic to enchant;
> And my ending is despair
> Unless I be relieved by prayer,
> Which pierces so that it assaults
> Mercy itself, and frees all faults.
> As you from crimes would pardoned be,
> Let your indulgence set me free.

## THE END